What people are saying about ..

Matthew Paul Turner

"Matthew Paul Turner's breezy, warm, conversational style should especially endear him to those under thirty-five. Turner is one of Christianity's fresh voices in the tradition of Rob Bell, Brian McLaren, and Donald Miller."

Publishers Weekly

"Matthew proves that learning the real truth about Jesus can be raw, witty, and redemptive. His broken but magical journey has enriched my own."

Bebo Norman, recording artist

"Matthew Turner is gutsy, raw, and relevant. He has a way of taking a tongue-in-cheek tone with his writing and polishing it with compassion and insight instead of bitterness and angst."

Cameron Strang, president and CEO of Relevant Media Group

"Matthew Paul Turner is a benchmark on our morning show. The audience has come to love his information, his fun-loving interaction with our team, and the great love of Christian music he brings to our show."

Danny Clayton, The Fish radio station, Milwaukee, Wisconsin

"Matthew Turner is a groundbreaking voice in music journalism. His refreshing style of sculpting a story is captivating and daring. He leaves behind the trite and digs deep to find the substance in his subjects. Features written by Matthew are on the level of *Rolling Stone, Entertainment Weekly,* or *Vanity Fair*. A true leader in his field, I expect Matthew will be a force of change in the future of our industry."

Jaci Velasquez, award-winning recording artist

"Matthew Turner is relevant and understands culture, which enables him to connect to a variety of audiences. Matthew has a comfortable, down-to-earth style and makes a great effort to engage audiences. He has an awesome way of connecting with people and tackling real issues within the music industry."

J. D. King, executive director of Lifest

"I've worked with Matthew Turner for a number of years and continue to be amazed at his passion for the music industry. On a personal level, I have watched him grow in his walk with the Lord and have seen him stand up for his beliefs—even when it meant risking the approval of others. Matthew is a true disciple."

Janet Chismar, senior editor of Crosswalk.com

"Matthew is young, energetic, unpretentious, and full of fresh ideas that relate well to the college market."

Rebecca Chappell, communications professor at Anderson University

RELEARNING Jesus

How Reading the Beatitudes One More Time Changed My Faith

Matthew Paul Turner

RELEARNING JESUS
Published by David C. Cook
4050 Lee Vance View
Colorado Springs, CO 80918 U.S.A.

David C. Cook Distribution Canada
55 Woodslee Avenue, Paris, Ontario, Canada N3L 3E5

David C. Cook U.K., Kingsway Communications
Eastbourne, East Sussex BN23 6NT, England

David C. Cook and the graphic circle C logo
are registered trademarks of Cook Communications Ministries.

LCCN 2009920394
ISBN 978-1-4347-6794-3

First edition published by Revell under the title *Beatitude: Relearning Jesus through Truth, Contradiction, and a Folded Dollar Bill* in 2006
© Matthew Paul Turner, ISBN 978-0-8007-3093-2

The Team: Andrea Christian, Amy Kiechlin, Jack Campbell, and Caitlyn York
Cover Design: BIG Creative Team

Printed in the United States of America
Second Edition 2009

1 2 3 4 5 6 7 8 9 10

122908

contents

introduction

On the day I read Matthew 5 for what I can only imagine was the 857th time, I was drinking something that resembled coffee. But it wasn't coffee. By the time it had been blended together with ice, chocolate, caramel, and heavy cream and then topped with something white, whipped, and sweet, the flavor of coffee had pretty much been masked.

At the time, that was the only way I liked it.

I'm sure I appeared very "evangelical" that day to all who noticed me in the coffeehouse. My big green Bible was wide open and placed neatly out on the round table in front of me. I had it open to Matthew 5 because I desperately needed to hear from Jesus. For a while, I had become convinced that he wasn't speaking to me—or at least I wasn't able to hear him. I blamed his silence on my sporadic bouts with pornography.

But God had never been silent before. Not to me. For most of my life, he and I had carried on seemingly endless conversations. So, I was learning firsthand how much I hated those times when he refused to talk. It had been five days since I had last looked at porn, a guilt-inducing experience that had left me feeling fearful and desperate. Almost immediately after I had finished looking, I began asking him for forgiveness. And that was when I got the silent treatment.

A friend said I should read Matthew 5. "God always speaks to me when I read Matthew 5," he said. I had read this passage many times, and every time I reread it, I would certainly learn something new. But the 857th reading of Matthew 5 changed my life. It helped put me back on the path, a path that I had begun walking a few years before. It was a trail that would eventually lead me to change the way I live my life.

These are the words I read:

> When Jesus saw his ministry drawing huge crowds, he climbed a hillside. Those who were apprenticed to him, the committed, climbed with him. Arriving at a quiet place, he sat down and taught his climbing companions. This is what he said:
>
> "You're blessed when you're at the end of your rope. With less of you there is more of God and his rule.
>
> "You're blessed when you feel you've lost what is most dear to you. Only then can you be embraced by the One most dear to you.
>
> "You're blessed when you're content with

just who you are—no more, no less. That's the moment you find yourselves proud owners of everything that can't be bought.

"You're blessed when you've worked up a good appetite for God. He's food and drink in the best meal you'll ever eat.

"You're blessed when you care. At the moment of being 'care-full,' you find yourselves cared for.

"You're blessed when you get your inside world—your mind and heart—put right. Then you can see God in the outside world.

"You're blessed when you can show people how to cooperate instead of compete or fight. That's when you discover who you really are, and your place in God's family.

"You're blessed when your commitment to God provokes persecution. The persecution drives you even deeper into God's kingdom.

"Not only that—count yourselves blessed every time people put you down or throw you out or speak lies about you to discredit me. What it means is that the truth is too close for comfort and they are uncomfortable. You can be glad when that happens—give a cheer, even!—for though they don't like it, *I* do! And all heaven applauds. And know that you are in good company. My prophets and

> witnesses have always gotten into this kind of trouble.
>
> "Let me tell you why you are here. You're here to be salt-seasoning that brings out the God-flavors of this earth. If you lose your saltiness, how will people taste godliness? You've lost your usefulness and will end up in the garbage.
>
> "Here's another way to put it: You're here to be light, bringing out the God-colors in the world. God is not a secret to be kept. We're going public with this, as public as a city on a hill. If I make you light-bearers, you don't think I'm going to hide you under a bucket, do you? I'm putting you on a light stand. Now that I've put you there on a hilltop, on a light stand—shine! Keep open house; be generous with your lives. By opening up to others, you'll prompt people to open up with God, this generous Father in heaven."
>
> —Matthew 5:1–16

On that day, those familiar words weighed heavily on my heart and mind. They seemed more potent to me than before, like God was actually trying to tell me something. I felt numb.

As soon as I finished reading, I put my forehead down against my Bible's green faux leather cover. I sat there with my eyes closed and my head against the face of my Bible. I'm not sure what the people behind the counter thought of me. And I didn't care.

For thirty-two minutes, I said nothing. I thought about nothing. I did nothing. I just remained quiet and still. Music played over the speakers, but I couldn't tell you what songs. People sat down in the chairs that were near to me, but I ignored them and didn't care what they were thinking about me. If God was going to speak, I wanted to make sure I heard exactly what he was going to say.

When I lifted up my head and opened up my eyes, God made one thing clear. He gave me a verse. It wasn't much. He didn't sit down and have a conversation with me. He didn't leave a message on my Facebook wall. But somehow I knew he wanted me to rethink these specific words:

> You're blessed when you get your inside world—your mind and heart—put right. Then you can see God in the outside world.

As I stood up quickly to leave the coffeehouse, I picked my Bible up off the table, and the top left-hand corner of it hit my cold chocolate coffee drink. I watched as its contents splattered all over everything that was anywhere near me. Everywhere I looked I saw a brownish milky substance with chunks of deflated whipped cream. The frothy mixture spilled all over the nicely painted floor, the expensive chairs, the table with a checkerboard painted in the middle, and one of the other customers.

"Oh sir, I am *so sorry!*" I exclaimed with as much feeling as I could.

The man, who was dressed in a sport coat and a pair of seventies-looking dress pants, stood up as fast as he could to miss the rest of the drink pouring down from the side of the table.

"Crap!" I said. "Again, sir, I am *so* sorry."

"Don't worry about it, boy," said the man nicely. "Honestly, I am just glad to know that you're alive."

We were both on our hands and knees, cleaning up the mess with small napkins.

"What?"

"I'm not kidding," said the kind man seriously. "You sat there with your head against your Bible for so long that I was very close to shaking you or calling 9-1-1. I didn't know what to think."

"Oh, I was just being still. I am sorry that I got coffee all over you."

"It's OK."

It took me nearly fifteen minutes to get all of the coffee wiped up.

"Well, sir, I am leaving; thank you so much for helping me clean up the mess."

"Oh, no problem. I'm used to helping clean up messes. My dad always said, 'Cleanliness is next to godliness.'"

The man paused for moment.

"I always hated that stupid little saying."

"Why?" I asked.

"Because it doesn't mention one thing about all of the hard work and all the crap you have to go through to get things clean."

As the man laughed, I realized how much cleaning I had to do.

Pause and Reflect

When you read Matthew 5, is there a particular phrase that speaks to you?

When you consider the words “You’re blessed when you get your inside world—your mind and heart—put right,” what do they mean to you?

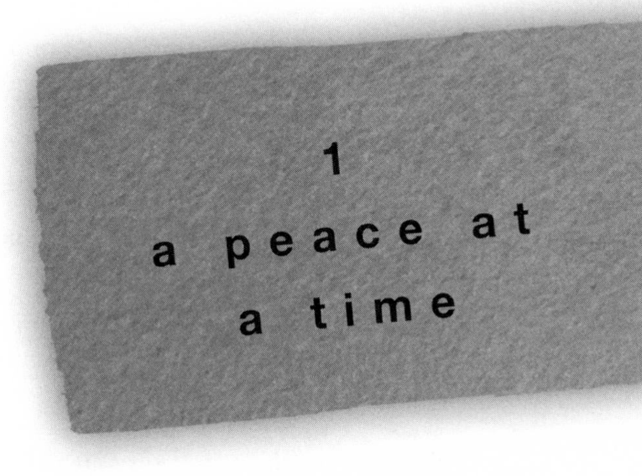

Nonviolence means avoiding not only external physical violence but also internal violence of spirit. You not only refuse to shoot a man, but you refuse to hate him.

—Martin Luther King Jr.

Blessed are the peacemakers, for they will be called sons of God. (Matt. 5:9 NIV)

—Jesus

BLESSED ARE …

The Sermon on the Mount is a mouthful. The words of Jesus bewilder me sometimes. Seriously, blessed are the peacemakers? What was he thinking? There are few things more difficult for me than making peace, keeping peace, or even pursuing peace. I'm much better at creating mayhem or stirring up trouble or writing recipes for calamity. But peacemaking? That's not one of my natural talents. Why couldn't Jesus have made it easier for us humans? For instance, why couldn't he have said, "Blessed are the selfish"? That I could handle.

But Jesus didn't make it easy. In fact, nothing I read in Matthew 5 seems simple. But when he said, "Blessed are the peacemakers," he raised his expectation for humanity. And when I consider this world or even how I live my own life, I can't help but wonder if he raised the bar too high.

As difficult as it might seem, Jesus wanted the people of his time to live their lives as conduits of peace. And not just any kind of peace—his kind.

When Jesus first spoke those words, I can only imagine how many blank and awkward stares he got from the crowd. Sure, there were probably people sitting on that mountainside who were awestruck and humbled by his words—probably many of them. But I can't help but believe there could have been a few who didn't know what to think about Jesus at first. There had to be some people who were thinking to themselves, *What is Jesus talking about? This guy's a good speaker, but he's saying all kinds of things that go against the teaching of Moses and Elijah.* Others may have said, "This man's nothing but a bloody liar." (I imagine that last guy with a British accent.)

Of course, I can't be certain that there were hecklers and skeptics at the Sermon on the Mount. But I know how the messages of Jesus rub people the wrong way today; I can only imagine they must have done the same back then—even at the beginning of his ministry. One thing I do know is that every time I think about—*really* think about—his call for me to be a peacemaker, I get annoyed; I get angry;

I get frustrated. *Why?* I get this way because no matter what I am doing—good or bad—the words of Jesus rub up against my human nature. They are like salt against my freshly overbitten fingernails. Peacemaking is some of the hardest living I have ever had to do.

There are certainly times when I wish that Jesus had said, "Blessed are the selfish."

The Peace Sign

Jayden, a good friend of mine, has been an activist against the war in Iraq since it began in 2003. Long before hating the war was popular, my friend was proudly in the minority. Whether I agree with her point of view or not, it's hard to argue with someone who has her kind of passion. She demonstrates it beautifully by simply believing wholeheartedly in her cause. My friend loves the idea of peace more than any person I know.

Even though, in my not-too-often-humble opinion, she and her peace friends go a little overboard once in a while (and I've told her that, too), we've come to a mutual understanding. We don't always agree on politics and such, but we are determined not to let our social differences disrupt our personal love for each other. And between you and me, she's sometimes kind of hard to get along with.

But despite the work it sometimes takes to be friends, I have a lot of respect for the uphill struggle my friend is involved in on behalf of peace. She goes to meetings about peace, makes phones calls to voters about peace, and attends rallies to support peace. And I just love it when she goes to rallies. But I have a little confession to make: I look forward to her going to rallies, not because of her passionate stance and what she might accomplish, but because every time she attends one of her rallies, she always returns with hilarious, nonpeaceful stories.

On one occasion she returned from a rally with a story about one of the guys from her "peace club" throwing a bucket of paint at a police officer. Her friend, of course, was arrested. Another time, while marching in a nearby city, she and a friend of hers led the entire parade down the wrong street. Her peace friends were *furious.* In fact, a few of them got so mad that they left the rally right then and there. But my favorite story was the time she tripped and fell down right in front of a White House guard at the largest of all antiwar demonstrations. The guard, a large African-American man dressed in uniform, actually helped her up off the ground while the rest of her group continued its march. My friend eventually caught up with the others, but it was too late. They had already passed the spot where they got as close to the White House as the authorities would let them, and to her frustration, she missed out on meeting Martin Sheen.

Darn it.

Jayden thrives when she talks about peace, and she always has a new story or concern.

"Oh, I was so disgusted today, Matthew," she said to me a couple of years ago. When my friend tells stories, I like being in the same room. Phone conversations aren't nearly as fun. She gets very expressive. Her hands move up and down. Her face gets red. It's hard not to laugh a little when she gets hyperpassionate. And on this particular day, her emotion and passion were out in full force.

"You will *not* believe this, Matthew," she said. "There we were, trying to have a peace rally, a *peace* rally, mind you, when all of a sudden about fifty people from who the heck knows where begin forcing their way through the police line. It was awful. I got sprayed with some kind of police gas; lucky for me, I had my back turned, so it hit *and stained* my jacket. And I wasn't even doing anything wrong. It was all of these other people rushing the line. I was trying to spread peace, and they were making a ruckus. I'm almost positive it was a bunch of right-wingers trying to make our peace rally go sour. It had to be … and of course, the news cameras only cover the *crazies*. Oh, it turned into a *huge* mess."

"That sounds *very* peaceful," I said, hints of sarcasm seeping through my tone. "I'm sure sorry I missed that."

She just glared at me.

"Well, did anyone read your sign?" I asked, trying to change the subject. She had taken a great deal of time to create this rather cleverly designed sign that read, "GIVE US PEACE IN THE MIDDLE EAST, HELP US STOP THE BEAST!" Believe me, I wish you could have seen that sign; I promise that the design was much more impressive than the slogan.

"Yes, a few people read it; I think a *Washington Post* photographer took a picture of me holding it. So, maybe I'll get close to the dream of what every peace activist longs for: I'll be on the front page tomorrow morning," she said, mocking herself. My friend then looked at me as though something were terribly wrong. "Can I ask you a question?"

"Sure."

"Do you think I'm crazy for doing this kind of stuff?"

"No. Why would you think that?"

"Are you sure?"

"I don't think you're crazy," I said seriously. "You're doing something you believe in, and I respect that. Now, I don't always think something 'peaceful' comes out of those kinds of things. I'm just not sure you can *rally* for peace. That's all."

"I know, Matthew; maybe you're right. Today was just awful."

"Do you think you helped the cause for peace today?" I asked.

"No, I don't think we did," she said. "I don't think one person was influenced by what we did today. Not one."

"But aren't you missing the point?" I asked. "Isn't the point of a peace rally to simply let the government know that you disagree with the way they are handling things?"

"I honestly don't know what the point is; I've just always done it—ever since I was in college," she said, laughing. "President Bush wasn't even at the White House today. So he didn't hear us."

"I'm sure Karl Rove will give him the message," I replied.

She stuck her finger in her mouth and pretended to gag.

"Let me ask you a question," I said. "Do you think Jesus would *ever* be at a peace rally?"

"I don't know. I mean, he was the ultimate peace*maker*. But I think if he were to come to one, he'd have something to say about how we actually do it. Do you think he could find a way to make twenty thousand people be peaceful? I'm telling you, it's hard work, especially when we're all screaming, 'We want peace! We want peace!'"

"I'm sure he'd never go," I said.

"Why not?"

"It just doesn't seem to be his kind of peace."

"I think it is," she said with confidence. "So do you think I'll be on the cover of the *Washington Post* tomorrow morning?"

"Maybe. It would be kind of fun."

Thoughts on War and Peace

I have had many conversations with Jayden (and other friends too) about protesting war and how it relates to the peace that Jesus asks us to make. But as much as my friends think they're fighting the good fight of faith when they protest, I'm pretty sure that the peace that gets yelled for and turned into clever slogans at peace rallies is not the kind of peace Jesus talks about.

When I lived in the Washington DC area, I saw several peace rallies. Watching them over the years, I became convinced that the peace demanded during those wartime gatherings is a one-dimensional type of peace. In other words, in nearly every case I witnessed, protestors were just looking for the kind of peace that gets one side (or both) to drop their weapons and retreat or not go to war at all. This is a type of peace, but it isn't the peace Jesus described.

The peace Jesus talks about doesn't come in the form of agreements or treaties or rallies. The type of peacemaking Jesus refers to in the Beatitudes is not simply about giving up; it's not about dropping weapons and returning home. I must admit, that kind of "peacemaking" would be a lot simpler. If all we had to do was wave a white flag in an effort to reveal that we've surrendered, I think more people would do it. But deep down, most people know in their hearts that peace is a lot more than silencing guns and harsh words.

It's certainly a good step when guns stop firing and people stop dying. But an act of surrender doesn't mean that peace has arrived. It just means somebody has given up. Giving up doesn't mean they're at peace. Laying down weapons, whether they are guns or words or fists, is a good first step toward knowing peace. But it's not the whole picture.

Brother Andrew addresses the concept of peace in his book *Light Force*. Writing about his experiences in the Middle East, he makes an argument that's intriguing to a lot of people but controversial to many more. He suggests that true peace is not possible anywhere, in any situation, under any circumstances, without Jesus. Treaties do not bring true peace. Wars do not bring true peace. There is no *true* peace without Jesus. It's impossible. Brother Andrew reminds us that the Bible calls Jesus the Prince of Peace. If he's the *Prince* of all things peaceful, surely he is needed in a situation for peace to even be an option (Brother Andrew and Al Janssen, *Light Force: A Stirring Account of the Church Caught in the Middle East Crossfire*. Grand Rapids: Revell, 2005).

I struggle with that idea, mostly because I want peace to be possible everywhere. I want the Iraq War to be over. I want Israel and Palestine to get along. I want Democrats and Republicans to work together for the good of our country. But I also know what it takes for there to be peace between my wife and me. Peace is hard to come by.

In most cases, we humans really don't have a clue what peace is like. We have an idea—an idea that gets presented to us by historians, the media, and others. But I've learned that if I want to have any chance at being a maker of peace in the world around me and in my personal life, I have to *know* peace when I see it.

Before my journey began, I only knew when I didn't see it.

A BIGGER LESSON ABOUT PEACE*MAKING*

When Jesus was here on earth, he was the greatest of peacemakers. He achieved a popular following because he made peace by calming seas, casting out demons, and healing broken hearts. When he brought peace into people's lives, he wasn't simply ending their painful circumstances. In other words, he didn't just help them out of their problems—he made them whole again. Those people Jesus impacted experienced a fullness they had never imagined was possible. That's what the peace of Jesus is about—filling up a person and making him or her whole. But is that kind of peace possible for everyday people like ourselves?

It's easy for Jesus to do such things. He only had to walk into a situation, and peace would occur if he deemed it appropriate. He didn't have to say anything or do anything miraculous; many times his presence was enough to bring peace and calm to the lives he touched and the situations he encountered. His life on earth was about bringing wholeness to the lives of people.

In *The Message*, Eugene Peterson actually uses the word *wholeness* in spots where other translations use *peace*. The word *wholeness* implies that the peace we pursue through Jesus—as well as the peace we *make* through Jesus—is always about reconciliation.

It's about a human being finding true completion.

Peacemaking is not simply about having working relations between two countries or two entities or two people. Sure, that might be a small part of what Jesus was trying to communicate, but like most of his core messages, the peacemaking that he talks about has more to do with the condition of human hearts. He doesn't expect us to *just* put down our guns; we have to take many more actions for peace to be possible. He knows that out of a person's heart come actions. Those actions are a reflection of what's going on inside of us. It's the old "what goes up must come down" theory, but this time it's "what's inside will eventually come out."

Throughout history, world leaders have struggled to balance the relationship between war and peace. It's easy to look back over history and remember the great wars. Wars stick out in history like large black blotches on white paper. Memory is long when peace is unavailable or fails to exist. Jesus knew that about nonpeace; he knew that the stench of unrest and war wreaks havoc on a society's well-being. But the struggle to make peace is not a macro problem. It almost always begins with an individual heart.

As we know all too well, peace is a struggle for humanity in general, in all levels of life—work, family, and relationships. Wherever people exist, finding peace is problematic. And so often, just as a glance back in history reminds us quickly of our ancestors' mistakes, we often see that the most vivid memories in our own personal history are ones where peace is nowhere to be found. This is true in my own life, at least. In fact, it has been within the confines of Christian culture that I have suffered the most effects of nonpeace.

Pause and Reflect

Do you know someone who has actively pursued being a peacemaker?

How do you think your current understanding of peace is different from Jesus' understanding of peace?

Peace, Love, and Christians

Sadly, it's hard for me to remember a time when my father would not come home from the deacons' meetings at our church angry, frustrated, or confused. My dad had been a deacon at our church for as long as I could remember. As I scan the memory of my childhood faith, I find it difficult to remember a peaceful meeting occurring among those seven men who had been voted in by the church membership to manage the direction of the church. They struggled to get along.

The majority of those seven men, men I respected as an upstanding, ten-year-old, born-again Christian, quarreled more than led. If it wasn't the pastor, it was the building fund. If it wasn't how the church's money was being spent, it was the politics of the church. Sure, the men treated each other with respect when they were in front of the church body, but behind closed doors, issues and religiosity separated them.

When I knew that my dad was having a Thursday night deacons' meeting, my little heart and head would swell with anxiety. Often my mom, sisters, and I would gather in a circle and pray for my dad to have wisdom and patience in those meetings. But more often than not, our prayers seemed to remain unanswered. If my father was quiet when he walked through the door, we knew that it probably didn't go too well.

In seventh grade, one of my closest and dearest friends since grade school left my church's Christian school without saying goodbye. One day, out of the blue, her name was called over the speaker. She gathered her belongings and never walked into our classroom again. Before that day, her father, one of the biggest men I had ever seen, had been one the deacons. However, a disagreement among the men on the deacon board caused him to take action—he left the church angrily, pulled his kid from the school, and never stepped foot in the church again. I've only spoken to that old friend a couple of times since she left the school that day. The last time we chatted, it had been seven years since that event had occurred, and she was still living her life somewhat impacted by the pain she felt from my church. And honestly, as crazy as this might sound, sometimes I still feel the pain of that day too.

That day, I believe, was my first experience in which the lack of peace within the walls of the church had very personal repercussions. It hurt to lose a friend. When Alicia left the school that day, it caused disruption among my friends and me. Kids said mean things about my father, the pastor, and the rest of the leaders. People took sides. Some left the church. Others pretended the problem didn't exist. "We need to move on," I remember many saying. And back then, I probably would have thought they were right; we did need to move on. But in the process of relearning Jesus, I realized that moving on without peace is not moving on at all.

Today, when I talk to my dad about those years at that church, he shakes his head in disgust. My father, who has been a follower of Jesus for nearly forty years, has told me many times that the "Lord's work" has aged him more than any other part of life. Some of his most difficult experiences in life have been when he was surrounded by Christians—Christians who couldn't get along. I find that so saddening. But my dad is not alone in that experience. I've met many people of faith throughout my lifetime who would say that the effort they have put into "Christian" work has brought them more pain and frustration than peace. So many look back on their spiritual pasts and see more big black blotches of unrest than they see peace.

As followers of Jesus, we should be leading the crusade toward peace. That's why listening to people tell me these kinds of stories leaves me feeling overwhelmed. I often think: *How can we make peace in the world when we can't even make peace in our churches? If we indeed know Jesus, then why is peace within the walls of the church hard to come by?*

So, many times in my life, I have been a victim of nonpeace. But I've also been a perpetrator of it. I'm guilty of being the nonpeaceful man who is *inside* the church where the love of Jesus is supposed to "flow like a river." Many times, I make things worse instead of more peaceful, causing the people I love alarm and worry.

I believe peace evades me because I fail to keep running back to the source of peace. And unless I have an ongoing connection with that source, the peacemaking that Jesus talks about is impossible.

Pause and Reflect

How do you pursue peace? Do you believe it's even possible?

Have you encountered peace in this world? If so, what was that like?

From your perspective, how does Jesus bring peace into somebody's life?

PEACEFUL POSSIBILITIES IMAGINED

"Matthew!"

My wife was yelling my name down the hallway—*again*. She doesn't do it too often, but when she does, I almost always know that I have done something stupid with the laundry.

My wife is a saint for putting up with the process that she has had to endure to debachelorize me. (That's still a journey too.) And when it comes to doing the laundry, I can be as dumb as they come. Now, I do know the difference between whites and darks, but I don't like rules, so I occasionally will put a couple of *my* white things in with the dark stuff. I don't care about having blue-tinted boxer-briefs. But that was *not* the problem this time around.

Usually, the big crisis that happens between my wife and me stems from my not cleaning out the pockets of my jeans. I've washed a lot of money, business cards, and receipts in my day. One time I left an ink pen in the dryer and got blue ink all over everything. My wife's favorite bra had huge blue blotches on it. I thought it looked all right, but she didn't think so. Another time, I left mustard packets from McDonald's in my shorts' pockets and put them in the washing machine.

But on that day, Jessica was yelling my name because I had left my wet green towel draped across the door to our bedroom. Not that big of a deal, right?

When I was single, the door was where my towel felt at home. Sure, it looked sloppy, but being a single adult for nearly twelve years had brought me a few "nonmarriageable" habits. I was *young* in marriage; I was still learning. I still *am* learning. And Jessica is quite good at keeping me on that journey.

"Why do you insist on putting your towel on the door?" said my wife in a loud but forceful tone. I could tell she was serious.

"Why is it a big deal? Why can't you just work through it?" I retaliated. *Yeah, so that statement didn't go over too well.*

"*Work through it?* Why can't *you* work through it? Why can't you put your towel in the clothes hamper where it is supposed to go, or on the rack next to the shower?"

She had a point there, and I knew it. But I still wasn't willing to back down—not quite yet. I still had a few more good points in me, too.

"Jessica, you're making a mountain out of a molehill. Why does it *really* matter if my towel is on the door or if it's in the hamper? *I like it on the door! Do you have to change everything about my life?*"

Yeah, so that statement didn't go over too well, either. My lovely wife just stared at me with a "you *did not* just go there" look on her face. Words couldn't say what we were feeling about each other at that particular moment. So, we did what comes naturally to us when we're not in the mood to make peace: We retreated to separate corners of the house. I walked about three feet into our living room and dropped down as loudly as I could onto the couch. She turned around and walked two and a half steps into our bedroom.

Sometimes the simplest situations are the hardest to make peaceful. At that point, when my wife and I were as far apart as a thousand-square-foot condo would allow, one of us was going to have to give in if peace was going to be an option. One of us was going to have to admit that the other was right. Someone was going to have to get humble.

But following Jesus in this life had taught me that simply giving in and admitting the other was right would only produce a *chance* for peace. It would not guarantee peace. Peace required one of us to sacrifice, drop our pride, rid ourselves of our selfishness, and then make a change in our behavior. And then, *maybe*, wholeness would become a possibility.

As I sat on my couch, alone in my living room, I deliberated with God. Actually, there was very little deliberating going on; he was pretty much putting me in my place. So I sat there, listening to God completely rip my "towel on the bedroom door" case to shreds. It sucks when you can't get the Savior of the world to be on your side. And from experience, I have learned that there is never anything remotely fun about being God whipped.

Finally, after calming down, I was ready to admit that I was the one who could (and should) make peace possible. So, I went to my wife and apologized, and I told her that it was me who was wrong. But apologizing was only the first step; I couldn't stop there. I also had to promise that the necessary changes would be made in my lifestyle to ensure that the towel would never be left on the bedroom door in the future.

I can't tell you how hard that was for me.

That event happened more than three years ago. And still, to this day, every single time I jump out of the shower and finish drying off, I still have the urge to just throw my towel over the door. I *don't* do it, but gosh, I am tempted.

Making peace, even in the small areas of life, is hard. But I believe that when we're peaceful in the small things, somehow God uses those circumstances to teach us how to also make peace in the big areas of life too.

Perhaps because of my childhood church experience, I ended up with a very bleak view of peacemaking. To be completely honest, I just didn't know how to do it. On the journey, Jesus taught me what making peace is about. He opened my eyes to the fact that I needed to learn that *peace*—his kind of peace—is about making a situation whole. It's not just about ending an argument. It's not simply about taking back the mean-spirited remarks. It's about humbling oneself enough to change. It's almost never easy to take on the attributes of Christ and present them in certain situations. But when we see it happen, it's an amazing event to witness.

A couple of years ago, I witnessed the peace of Jesus come into a very ugly situation involving a teenage girl and her youth pastor. I'm sure you can imagine the nature of the predicament, so there's no need to give much detail. Because of the sensitivity of this type of occurrence, reconciliation and peace are often not possible. In most situations such as these, parents of the victim become irate, and some would likely want to *kill* the youth pastor. And most people would feel as though the family's anger would be completely justified. And sadly, church leadership often doesn't know the best way to handle this kind of situation—some want to hide it; some offer a graceless conclusion.

However, in the terrible situation that I watched unfold, none of those things happened. I marveled as I watched a family's faith in Jesus allow them the ability to make peace not only an option in the life of this young youth pastor and their daughter; they actually walked into the situation demanding that it be the *only* option. Bringing the possibility of peace into that kind of situation must have been excruciatingly difficult. But the pastor, along with the mother, father, and daughter, worked through a long list of necessary steps to make it possible. All of the parties who were involved met together. They talked about the situation. Tears ensued. Apologies ensued. Forgiveness and grace ensued. And ultimately, over time, wholeness ensued.

I'm not sure if I have ever witnessed anything like it. In some ways, the ability to make peace in that situation seemed almost awkward. Do I understand that kind of peacemaking? Not really. But when I finally had a chance to stand back and consider the situation, I was left breathless with the love and forgiveness exhibited by that mother and father.

Jesus' entire goal was to bring wholeness to the lives of people. His mission for me is to take the same wholeness he gives me and apply it to the everyday situations I experience in life.

Being Conduits of Peace

I struggle with the idea of peace—mostly my role in making it, finding it, seeing it; peace isn't something that comes naturally to me. As with all things that Jesus teaches me on my journey, I've learned that peacemaking begins with getting out of the way. People who bring peace along with them tend to be people who are pursuing lives that aren't centered on themselves. Despite knowing Jesus, I have grown accustomed to centering life on me. Over the years, I have realized that my constant need to take care of me has inhibited my ability to be a peacemaker.

Getting out of the way is the hardest part of following Jesus. And sometimes, that's all he wants from us. He just wants us to get humble, and that's when he can use us. He's constantly having to remind me to "get out of the way, Matthew; I can't use you or the situation that you're in if you're going to only focus on your needs." It's never easy when Jesus shows you a vivid picture of yourself. His words do not candy-coat the truth. That kind of honesty is hard to take, but it's also needed for peace to breathe in a situation.

I've learned through experience that peacemaking is never simple. You have to be listening for Jesus' voice. And I am sure I miss him more than I hear him. But once in a while I do hear him loud and clear.

Three years ago, my friend Julie was in a confusing place in life. Over the course of several months, she had lost her job, been unable to find work, and consequently was experiencing some financial struggles. Her situation had made many (including me) believe that she might be battling through a bout with depression.

Julie and I have been friends since we were both three years old. Over the years, she has become more like a sister to me than a mere friend. For many years, the two of us were inseparable. When I heard from several mutual friends of ours that Julie was having a hard time, I made a point to get together with her the next time I was in my hometown.

On a late-summer afternoon, while sitting in my parents' glassed-in porch, Julie began to describe what she was feeling. She explained a little about where she was spiritually, mentally, and emotionally. I could see bits and pieces of hurt escaping through her words and her tears. It was obvious to me that her defense mechanisms were kicking in to protect her from feeling too beat up and depressed. Listening to Julie tell her story, I was sure that something was missing in her.

As Julie and I chatted that day, Jesus began speaking to me. It was through a simple nudge on my heartstrings, a hard-to-describe whisper in my spiritual gut. It wasn't a huge production; it was just a simple split-second thought that ran through my mind.

Bring peace to Julie's life; let her come live with you in Nashville.

When I felt those words in my heart, I figured it must have been a mistake. I assumed I must not have heard Jesus correctly. He couldn't have said that. Apparently, Jesus realized that I was struggling with doubt because he repeated his words:

Let Julie come live with you in Nashville.

How is that supposed to work, God?

You're going to sleep on the floor in the living room, and Julie is going to have your room. It won't be easy, but peace will come.

I panicked a little: *Julie come live with me? What is God thinking?* The idea seemed preposterous to me. She's a girl. I'm a boy. *We're not married!* What would that look like? But I was almost positive that I heard God correctly. In the back of my mind, I was thinking about how I had always been told that Jesus frowned on guys and girls living together—you know, the whole "appearance" of evil.

Afraid that I had heard God wrong, I decided I would talk to my mother. If my mom said no, I'd know that my fiancée would say no too. Oh yeah, I forgot to mention that I was *engaged*. At that point, I was pretty convinced Jesus was *out of his mind*.

That evening, after talking with Julie, I asked my mom about Jesus' crazy little idea. I expected her to think it was an absolutely ridiculous concept; how could she think otherwise? So, that night, while Mom was doing the dishes (she's a little easier to convince when she's doing something), I popped the question.

"*I think that's a wonderful idea*," my mother said.

Her positive response shocked me.

"Matthew, I think that might be the best thing for Julie! You definitely should!"

What?! I was floored that my mom, the stereotypical over-churched, conservative woman—minus the tendency to be an ugly dresser—was actually receptive to Jesus' idea. In fact, my mom didn't just think the idea was good; she *loved* the idea.

"You and Julie have been friends for years; she's like your sister. It's a perfect plan, and I think it will really help her."

But Mom's acceptance of the idea only meant that I *had* to talk with Jessica (then, my fiancée) about it, and I had no idea how she would respond. Later that night, over the phone, I posed the idea.

"Let me get this straight," said Jessica. "You want to let *Julie*, your best friend since you were three, sleep in your bedroom for three months? And you're going to sleep in the living room?"

"Umm, yeah," I said back to her. "I feel like God wants me to do this. But I won't do it unless I have your support."

"So, while I'm living seven hundred miles away from you, you're going to have your friend, *who is a girl*, living with you?"

"*Riiiight.*"

"And you're sure this idea is from God?"

"I believe it is."

"Truthfully, I'm not too excited about it," she said. "But if you think it's what Jesus wants you to do, I'll support you through it. I might not always be happy about it, but I'll always support you, Matthew Paul Turner."

I knew with all my heart that Jessica meant that—*all of it.* Whenever she calls me by my full name, she *really* means what she is saying. Not only did she believe in me, but I was certain that deep down inside her heart, she also hated the idea. But she was willing to give peace a chance.

So, one month later, Julie moved in. And I have to be honest—it wasn't always easy. In fact, at times, it was downright difficult. But the change in scenery and people and church life brought peace to Julie's life. I was simply a conduit of the peace that Julie needed to find in Jesus. I don't say that proudly; I simply recognize the truth that I heard Jesus correctly that afternoon on the porch.

Sometimes, in order to live the way Jesus intends for me to live, I have to break a few rules. They're not always my rules. Sometimes they're the rules of a particular church. Sometimes they're the rules of friends or family. Sometimes they're simply rules that I have assumed to be true all of my life. But when I'm engaged in the journey, Jesus often surprises me by breaking a few rules.

When you're following after Jesus with abandon, you never quite know what you'll experience. Sometimes it will be a quiet, scenic ride, and at other times you may have to risk, having no idea what is ahead. As Michael Caine's character says in the movie *The Weather Man*, "The harder thing to do and the right thing to do are usually the same thing."

It more often than not seems to be that way for me. Jesus walks into my life and makes me do a lot of hard things, things that I frankly don't understand some of the time. But I know that for my friend Julie, that hard thing helped her find peace. And at the end of the day, helping somebody find a little peace brings you peace, too. Sure, my simple actions are not ridding the world of war or famine or the other things in life I wish would go away. But when I'm helping someone experience the presence of Jesus through peace, I'm letting him work through me, and in the process I'm doing exactly what he intended for me to do. And perhaps I'm giving someone else a chance to experience a little bit of the magic Jesus does in the lives of humans.

Peace Out

From time to time, I see my protesting friend online. She's still passionately rallying for peace every chance she gets. Despite not exactly understanding the method to her madness, I told her I was still very proud of her. I also admitted that her love of peace had actually put me on my own journey toward trying to be more intentional with peacemaking. But I told her that I was doing it a little differently—the rally I have going on is not on the streets of Washington DC; instead, it's going on inside my head and my heart.

"I bet you I know who showed up at that peace rally," she wrote, trying to be smart.

"LOL," I wrote back. "Yeah, Jesus showed up with a *big* sign that said, 'I AM PEACE; I AM PEACE. I AM HERE TO KILL THE BEAST.'"

"Ha-ha. Very funny! You shouldn't make fun."

"☺"

2
you are the salt of the earth

Nobody likes having salt rubbed into their wounds, even if it is the salt of the earth.

—Rebecca West

Let me tell you why you are here. You're here to be salt-seasoning that brings out the God-flavors of this earth. If you lose your saltiness, how will people taste godliness? You've lost your usefulness and will end up in the garbage. (Matt. 5:13)

—Jesus

SALT LICK

My entire family was excited that my grandmother was preparing one of her famous hot milk cakes for my seventh birthday party.

I loved my grandmother's hot milk cakes; she always smothered them with homemade caramel frosting. On the day of my birthday party, she had worked the better part of the afternoon making my cake. And the finished product looked beautiful. As the family sang "Happy Birthday" to me later that evening, my mother walked out into the dining area with my candlelit birthday cake and placed it right in front of me. My taste buds danced just thinking about my grandmother's cake.

When they finished singing, I took a deep breath, made a wish, and blew out the seven candles. Everyone applauded. My mom pulled the candles out of the cake. She began to cut the cake into slices and put each slice on my special Flintstone happy birthday plates. My sister piled two scoops of vanilla ice cream next to each piece. And then she handed the plates out to the rest of the family.

My aunt Jean got the first piece. She quickly and excitedly poked her fork into the cake and took a mouthful.

"Oh, my word!" exclaimed my aunt. She shook her head in disgust as she spit out the cake into her napkin. "*Mother!* What did you do to this cake?"

My aunt Jean's shocked tone alerted us all to stop what we were doing. Everyone in the room looked up. My mom stopped cutting slices of cake. My sister stopped serving the ice cream. I stared longingly at my cake and ice cream.

Perplexed by Aunt Jean's question, my grandmother took a small bite of her cake, then quickly grabbed the closest napkin and spit it back out.

"Oh, Jean," said my grandmother, with frustration in her voice. "It tastes like I put salt in the batter instead of sugar. How on earth did I make that mistake? The sugar container looks nothing like the salt container. I feel *horrible*."

Large tears welled up in her eyes as the weight of throwing a kink into my birthday gathering washed over her. My grandmother hated making mistakes like that; it reminded her that she was getting old and that her mind wasn't working like it used to.

I was only seven years old, but my Mammom and I were close. I loved her dearly. I walked over and gave her a big hug.

"Can we still eat your cake, Mammom?" I whispered in her good ear.

"My goodness, no, Matthew. I am so sorry; too much salt makes something like a cake taste awful."

Over the years, I have learned that salt is a very cumbersome ingredient. Too much salt ruins a lot more than just birthday parties.

Salt of the Earth

Jesus compares us, his followers, to salt. I like the concept of being compared to something as simple as salt. I'm not too sure what I would have thought if he had compared me to oregano or paprika or some other kind of notable spice rack commodity. I might have gotten used to the idea of being called the "paprika of the earth," but I'm not sure—mainly because I'm not convinced that paprika even has a purpose for being in my spice rack other than the fact that a little dash of it accents potato salad with a pretty red glow.

But the fact that I'm called to be like salt to the world enthralls me because, unlike curry or oregano, salt isn't a flavor—it's a substance used to enhance flavor. (Duh, right?) In most cases, we don't put salt on something to make it taste different; we put salt on something in hopes that it will help bring out the true flavor of whatever it is that's being eaten.

Jesus has taught me that he compares me to salt in order to give me an inkling of an idea of why I am here on earth. I'm not the flavor; I'm simply here to enhance the flavor. The "God-flavors," as Eugene Peterson so elegantly puts it, already exist here on earth; it's my job (and yours, too, if Jesus means something to you) as the "salt of the earth" to reveal his flavors, to bring them out, to enhance the Jesus experience for others. In other words, we live to bring more renown to God's existence in our everyday circumstances.

What I most love about this truth is that it means this: God is already here in the midst of whatever it is I will experience. I just need to help make him known. And when I make God known through seasoning the world around me with glimpses of his love and grace and mercy, I am doing exactly what I'm called to do.

I've learned that, unfortunately, just like in my grandmother's hot milk cake, too much salt overpowers all the other flavors. It takes over. Sometimes I have a tendency to bring my own version of Jesus into a situation, instead of recognizing that he is already there. Consequently, instead of enhancing Jesus, my words and actions become too much, and I end up making a potentially sweet piece of cake gross and bitter to the taste buds of others.

Sadly, too often I'm guilty of being a spiritual salt lick. On so many occasions, I have worn my faith so obtrusively that, when people see it, they perceive the idea of following Jesus as gross and unimaginable. The times I have ventured down this path, I fail to enhance the God-flavors of this world. Instead, my "salt" overwhelms, and usually some people are left with a very disgusting taste in their mouths.

Pause and Reflect

What do you believe Jesus was trying to tell us when he compared us to salt?

Do you know anybody you would describe as the salt of the earth?

AN EARLY LESSON IN BEING SALT

When I entered college in the fall of 1991, Jesus seemed to be more like a CEO to me than a father or friend or Savior. He was like Donald Trump, ready to fire me if I messed up. My Christian life during that time was systematic, built around an equation. I memorized a certain doctrine's vision statement; I followed its code of conduct and did my best to be a good employee of the Christian company of faith. My senior year in high school, I received "The Most Christ-Like Award." I guess you could say that I was employee of the year; I even got a plaque with my name on it. I hung it up in my room, right next to "The Pastor's Award" I had received the year before.

Today, that kind of thinking seems so very distant to me. The last seventeen years have shown me very different pictures of Jesus than those I held on to as a young college student. But despite all of the time and life that separate who I am today from that young believer I once was, sometimes I still feel the heartbreak of what that kind of spiritual enterprise left behind. Mainly, I think about the people I affected when I displayed to them my ugly, rigid version of Jesus. Sure, I was eventually able to break free of legalism, but when I think of the many disasters that I left in the path behind me as I held firmly and dependently to a skewed version of the truth, I can't help but ache for those I met along the way. (You'll read many stories in this book about that.) Over the years, I have often prayed for those poor individuals I tried to evangelize during that time.

While taking a business statistics class, I met Janet, who was a twenty-five-year-old lapsed Catholic, and Zachary, who was a twenty-year-old outspoken atheist. Before that class, I had never met an atheist, and I had been taught that all Catholics were going to hell. In my church, the word *Catholic* was derogatory. People would always frown or shake their heads in utter sadness if an individual said that he or she went to the Catholic church. When Janet informed me that she was Catholic, my heart sank as my mind drew up images of her soul burning in hell. But those images paled in comparison to what I thought about Zachary after he told me he didn't believe there was a God at all. In my mind, I linked him with all of the other people I believed were the great enemies of the Christian faith—Jezebel, the Philistines, JFK, and Hillary Clinton.

The experience of community college overwhelmed me at first. Because I had lived most of my young life inside the bubble of church, Christian school, and a church-centered family, I had never gotten a chance to see what happened on the "other" side. But at community college, I quickly found out. My first day there, I left the school in tears. I was overwhelmed by talk of drunken parties, hearing the f-word *three* times, and the fact that one of my professors was a "flaming liberal."

Although I had been spiritually programmed to respond to the "world's" challenges with scriptural answers, I felt rather unprepared and, quite frankly, out of my league. I had spent fifteen years studying under strict preaching. I was taught to be frank about my faith, intolerant of others' thoughts, and firm about holding true to my doctrinal belief system. My thoughts about Jesus and faith had never been challenged. So, when I was introduced to what I considered debauchery at Chesapeake College, I freaked.

"I'm *surrounded* by sinners," I told a friend of mine in utter desperation.

"Matthew, you will be surrounded by sinners for the rest of your life," he replied with pride. "Don't let them get the best of you. Just defend your faith. 'The word of God is sharper than any two-edged sword.' Use it."

My friend's words impressed me. I had learned many times that Christians were called to be the salt of the earth. My pastor had taught on that verse often. He said that the gospel message we're called to spread should burn the wounds of our enemies, and sometimes it would taste bitter to their lips. I went back to college believing that I needed to be prepared for any spiritual challenge that might come my way. And, over the next few weeks, I believed I had managed to prepare myself for "war." However, one conversation with Janet and Zachary proved otherwise.

"Why do you always have a Bible with you?" asked Janet one day after class.

"I like reading it between classes, so I keep it with me all of the time," I said. "We Christians believe that the Bible is the Word of God, so it's important that we know it."

Zachary laughed as he put his cigarette out on the cement steps where we were sitting. "It's just a bunch of stories, Matthew. Learn your history; there is absolutely no good evidence that supports that God 'inspired' that book. And by the way, it's one of the most poorly written books in history. I think it's folklore."

My heart raced as Zachary's words rubbed up against my doctrinal vision statement. I had always heard about people like Zachary, ones who believed that the Bible was simply a book of fairy tales, but I had never heard anyone say it out loud.

"Well, that's *your* belief," I replied. "And it's not *poorly* written. *Again*, that's your belief. And you might want to be careful how quickly you belittle the Word of God."

"I'm not the only one who believes that the Bible is a bunch of crap, Matthew," said Zachary, rolling his eyes and lighting up again. "In fact, some of the world's most intelligent people believe the Bible is nothing more than man's creation. I feel sorry for people like you—you're basing your entire life on stories that *never* happened."

The more he talked, the more his words made me sick to my stomach. It felt as though he had just poked me with a venomous needle and the poison was working its way through the rest of my body.

"These are not just stories!" I said in a whispered holler. "This is *God's Word*, whether you believe it or not. And besides, nothing you say is going to change my mind."

Janet flicked her cigarette against the building as hard as she could.

"Oh, would both of you just shut up? I'm sick of hearing it." Janet had been uncomfortably listening to the discussion that *she* had started. "I wish I had not even brought it up. We can believe what we want to believe; that's what makes the world go around. Let's leave it at that."

Zachary stared at the ground and just let his cigarette burn slowly.

I looked at Janet, thinking to myself that her kind of thinking was going to get her a one-way ticket to destruction. *What was I supposed to do? Was I going to let God's Word get mocked by some well-read atheist punk and a Catholic?*

"I got one more thing to add," I said nervously, but loudly. I looked at them intently, like a judge looks at a man he's getting ready to sentence to life in prison. "I pity you both. What are you living for? All I see is two people who are simply living for themselves. You think you're smart and you think you're cool, but when it comes to heaven or hell, all of that means absolutely nothing. Jesus said, 'I am the way, the truth, and the life.' *Period.* And I believe that if the two of you don't get saved and believe in Jesus, you'll live forever in—"

"OK, I've had enough!" said Janet, putting a book back into her bag. "I've been hearing that same stuff from my old fart of a priest since I was six years old ..."

I hardly heard what Janet was saying to me. I could feel my blood rushing away from my face as the feeling of embarrassment poured through every crevice of my body.

"... I don't believe it. I think if you're a good person you will get to heaven. And if I don't get to heaven, who cares? Hell is probably a whole lot more fun anyway."

Zachary looked at me and laughed. "You know what I believe, but thanks for the sermon."

They walked off together. I watched them as they made their way across the campus grounds, shaking their heads and continuing to laugh.

I was left there with one pounding thought: *My pastor was right; sometimes salt burns.*

I don't know where Janet and Zachary are now. I would love to have the chance to apologize for making the "cake" too salty. But I can't—that was fourteen years ago.

Christians Are Sometimes Weird

I'm not sure what it is about following Jesus that has made me act so weird and awkward and sometimes downright stupid. Is it because there are times when I *think* I know it all? Is it an inner need to make people understand me? But I'm not alone. Most of the weirdest things I have encountered in my life have "Christian" written on them. As in my case as a college student, the stench of Christians is revealed more through evangelism than anything else. I smell it often, the scent of misplaced words and poor, inexcusable timing. When mixed with uninterested patrons it becomes an especially nasty odor.

I was recently on a public bus in Denver. I was there on business, but one afternoon I managed to get away and see the downtown sights. While riding public transportation, I witnessed two local Colorado women stumble into a conversation with a thirtysomething businessman who was in Denver on business from Atlanta.

The conversation began as most conversations do—a friendly hello, a common interest in the weather, and a mutual love for something—this time it was for the city of Atlanta.

As I watched this conversation begin from my seat across the aisle, I couldn't help but eavesdrop. It's always fascinating for me to watch other people interact. Even before I knew where this conversation was heading, the fact that this clean-cut man was engaging in a conversation with two local women who looked as though they were on their way downtown for a few beers was a writer's dream come true.

After the "new friends" ended their chitchat, I noticed the man was pulling something out of his pocket. At the time, I wasn't sure what it was, but it was, to him, something important. Then, a couple of minutes later, the man cleared his throat and spoke, his tone nervous, as if he was unprepared for what he was about to say.

"So, can I ask you ladies a question? Are you two Christian women?" he asked. "I don't mean to be so forward, but …"

Wow. That was a gutsy question, indeed. And to me, it was quite unnecessary. I mean, from my vantage point, these two women had every stereotypical quality of lesbians. And they didn't seem like Jesus-loving lesbians. Their short, spiked hair was about as close to mullets as you can get and still be considered somewhat cool anywhere outside of West Virginia. Their clothes were masculine looking—baggy jean shorts and simple T-shirts. And one was still wearing her "Vote for Howard Dean" T-shirt despite the fact that W had won nine months prior. I would have bet a pretty good amount of money on the guess that the two women were *together*.

"No, we're not Christians," said the woman wearing the Howard

Dean T-shirt, laughing. She then looked at her friend and smiled. "We don't like religion too much."

Without skipping a beat, the businessman continued talking.

"Well, ladies, I know we don't have a lot of time, but I firmly believe I would be doing you a disservice if I didn't share with you my heart for Jesus," said the Christian man. "You see, I believe the Bible teaches that we are all sinners—"

"Sir," interrupted the woman who was *not* wearing the Howard Dean T-shirt, "we're really not interested in hearing this. We're not trying to be rude, but I think we'll both be OK without hearing your Jesus story."

The Christian man never blinked an eye. He looked down at the piece of paper that he had pulled out of his coat pocket and appeared to be scanning it quickly. He then spoke again.

"Well, if you would be so kind to just give me one more moment of your time, I would love to simply tell you why I believe in Jesus. You see, he is one day going to judge us all, ladies. And I don't believe it's going to be too long before it happens. It says in Romans 3 …"

I sat there worried for this man's life as he simply ignored these two women's request. They fidgeted. They stopped looking in his direction. They rolled their eyes toward me. They gave every indication that they wanted to be off the bus as quickly as possible. But he kept right on talking. And his knowledge of Scripture was impressive. He could seemingly quote many Bible verses that talked about our need for God's salvation.

"Sir," said the Howard Dean lover, "if you don't stop talking to us, we're going to move away from you. Can you please stop?"

"Yes, ma'am," said the businessman. "But let me give you this pamphlet on how you can learn more about being a Christian just in case you're interested. My phone number is at the bottom, and if you need ..."

Just as he was handing them the Jesus information he had pulled out of his pocket, the bus driver called the women's stop. I wasn't sure if it was *their* stop or if it was simply the *next* stop. They took the piece of paper and walked off the bus. One of them was laughing hysterically; the other was shaking her head in disgust. I watched them as they walked down the street. Miss "Howard Dean" took the Jesus information and tore it in two and threw it in a garbage can. Luckily, I don't believe the businessman saw that.

At the next stop, the businessman got off the bus. As he passed close by me, he handed me one of his pamphlets and said, "Glory to God. He's good, ain't he?"

Another person on the bus looked at me and called him a "nutcase."

He is a nutcase, I thought. But I felt guilty for thinking that.

When I experience events like this one, I want to run up to the would-be recipients and tell them that not *all* people who pursue loving Jesus are like this. I want to tell them that we think people like Pat Robertson and the folks on TBN are sometimes a little weird too. I would want them to know that we too see how God gets thrown into the cultural agenda—by politicians, preachers, and the like—to seemingly be used to promote an agenda or manipulate people.

But most of the time, almost every time, I remain silent, paralyzed by fear.

Walking with Jesus has taught me that I don't need to make those opinions known unless I'm talking to a very close friend. I believe if

I were to blurt those thoughts out to just anybody, it would be just as stench-stricken as obnoxious evangelism. I believe it would be hypocritical and conceited. I believe Jesus, in his power, takes care of situations where Christians add too much salt.

He's certainly had to take care of many situations where I have made him look foolish and ugly.

Pause and Reflect

Have you ever been guilty of forcing the gospel onto somebody, thinking that you're just doing what Jesus expects of you?

How do you believe Jesus has called you to be salt in the world around you?

SALT AGAINST THE TONGUE

I wish you could know Brian Bowdren. I met him in 1997.

Brian might be one of the most intriguing people I've had the pleasure of knowing. When I met him, he was forty-three and seemed almost perfect to me. There was something about Brian that made all who met him want to, and perhaps feel like they needed to, emulate his actions. People found something about him attractive.

Brian had an amazing job, one that took him all over the United States and to other parts of the world. His trips would often put him in front of high-profile people of influence, power, and wealth. Brian was talented and creative; his love of playing bass guitars led him to open a music shop in his quaint hometown on the Eastern Shore of Maryland, where he handcrafted bass guitars and sold them on eBay. Brian was in shape; he had a daily workout routine that kept his muscular body somewhere between 4 and 5 percent body fat. He was the sort of guy who made you kind of sick to your stomach.

Whenever I heard his wife, Cindy, talk about him, I had to stop and listen. Her love, respect, and adoration for her husband were something out of legend. She hated to be away from him. In fact, when our church would have weekend women's retreats, Cindy would go to the program during the day but never stay overnight. On one such occasion, I asked her why. Her reply made me smile. "Because I get to sleep next to Brian Bowdren; why would I ever want to miss a chance to do that?" she said with a coy grin.

Brian was an elder at his church. He was on the boards of several ministries. He was well-read. He played bass guitar in his church's praise and worship band. Most Christians who met him were surprised to learn that Brian had only come to know Jesus when he was in his midthirties. To many, that just didn't seem possible.

Brian was one of my bosses at a guitar shop/Christian coffeehouse called Jammin' Java. When I first met him, I wanted to have a job like Brian's. I wanted to be talented like Brian. I wanted a marriage like Brian's. But after spending three years watching this man's interaction with people, I wanted more than anything to bring out the God-flavors of the earth like Brian.

Brian lived out his faith by relating to people. I never once witnessed a person he couldn't relate to. When he would sit in board meetings with the elite of society, he was eloquent and masterful. Despite not being considerably *moved* or *impassioned* by his nine-to-five, that did not stop him from investing his complete self into his work and the relationships he created. He understood that his job was a part of the platform where Jesus wanted him to live out his faith. On a couple of occasions, I watched as some of the smartest and richest men and women of this world responded to Brian's good nature, love of life, and faith in someone much bigger than himself.

But Brian was far from one-dimensional. As we worked side by side at Jammin' Java, I witnessed Brian also relating to people who were much different from him—the poor, the unintelligent, the exotic, the liberal, and the outcasts. It didn't matter if he was talking to an atheist, a gothic-prone kid, or a dumb jock; Brian was always the same. He never once tried to talk over them or be condescending. His willingness to invest in people was uncanny to me. It was unrehearsed and never seemed forced. It was simply a part of who he was as a person, a person who was trying desperately to love Jesus. And he did that by loving people.

However, I believe it was in observing the relationships of those Brian loved the most that I realized what Jesus meant when he said, "You are the salt of the earth." I witnessed him shopping for dresses for his wife when there wasn't any holiday or anniversary to celebrate. On many occasions, Cindy would walk into church looking stunning. I'd tell her how pretty she looked that morning, and almost every time she would say, "Oh, I can't take any credit for this; Brian bought this for me."

"Was it for your birthday?" I'd ask.

"No, just because he loves me."

That was Brian.

I heard secondhand about how his words and wisdom helped our pastor during a difficult time. I watched him encourage his Sunday school class members to dive deeper in their faith. A friend of mine said that he wouldn't be playing drums if it weren't for Brian.

Another told me that he wouldn't have a relationship with Jesus if it weren't for Brian.

I'm actually pretty darn sure I wouldn't be writing this book if it weren't for Brian's investment in me. The manner in which Brian lived his life had a way of bringing out the best in people.

It saddens me that I have to write about Brian's life in the past tense. In December 2004, Brian died suddenly of unexplained causes. While working on a brand-new bass guitar that he had designed and created by hand, he collapsed. His wife discovered his body an hour or so later. An autopsy was performed, but it never explained the whys behind his early death. He was fifty.

Despite his passing, I still taste the God-flavors that Brian seasoned with his life on earth. Many do. But Brian wasn't perfect. He fought the same battles all of us do when we grapple with the idea of Jesus calling us salt. Staying out of God's way and allowing the mysteries of Jesus to shine through his life did not come naturally. Humility wasn't natural for him. Talking to the uneducated wasn't always simple for him. He wasn't *always* happy, and he didn't always have the perfect Jesus answer to offer people. Often surprising to me, he was overtly honest about not fully understanding everything about Jesus. Brian didn't believe he had to. To him, that was what faith was all about—believing in something he couldn't see. It seemed only logical to him that he would not be able to fully understand what he could not see with his eyes. To Brian, following Jesus wasn't about having all the answers; it was about simple obedience every day.

Brian felt the call to be salt in the world. One day, while we were drinking coffee and eating scones together, he looked at me with his humble eyes, and with his raspy voice he said, "Find the thread of Jesus in every story you live, Matthew.... We're not here to master this life; *we can't* master this life. We're here to use our own stories and journeys and struggles and joys to make those watching us see a glimpse of Jesus' story for their lives. I just try to live my life to the fullest." He seemed somewhat careful with his words. "And then I pray that God will use me in the story."

Brian laughed quietly and then added, "I know he doesn't need me, but it's always good fun to be a part of what God is doing in the lives of other people."

To those of us who still benefit from Brian's God story, the God-filled taste on our tongue is nothing less than beautiful.

Great beauty, great strength, and great riches are really and truly of no great use; a right heart exceeds all.

—Benjamin Franklin

Blessed are the pure in heart, for they will see God. (Matt. 5:8 NIV)

—Jesus

PURE AND SIMPLE

When I was a kid, my youth pastor made keeping one's heart pure sound pretty simple. "Deny the flesh," he'd tell us nearly every Sunday morning. "Be careful what your eyes see. Be careful what your ears hear." At thirteen, I believed my youth pastor was correct; staying pure was easy, especially when most of your world still revolved around getting to the next level of a Super Mario Brothers video game. But for some reason, getting older seemed to complicate all of that. It complicated it a lot, really.

Just before my sixteenth birthday, I was introduced to a whole new world of possibilities. On April 25, 1989, I got into the backseat of a beat-up blue driver's-ed car. A friend of mine and I were taking the driving class together. While I was waiting for my turn to practice driving on the highway, my friend took his turn behind the wheel. Our instructor, a Hispanic guy named Maurice, worked for his father, who owned and ran the driving school.

When we were finally safely driving on the highway, Maurice began looking through his tape collection for music to play. This excited me. It wasn't too often that I was able to listen to real music, especially the kind with guitar solos and drums. My church said guitar solos made Satan dance.

"How do you guys like your music?" asked Maurice with a wink.

"Um, I really don't know that much rock music," I replied. "So, you should just play whatever you want to play."

"Oh, whatever," said Maurice, pulling out one of his two hundred cassettes organized by release date in a huge carrying case. "You'll *definitely* know this song."

Maurice didn't get it. My friend and I were fundamentalist Baptists. We had been taught since we were five that his kind of music delivered us right into the hands of evil. We were supposed to run as fast as we could from such evil. But at the time, I chose to stay in the backseat.

"See if you guys know this song," said Maurice, shoving the tape into the player. He then turned his head toward me and gave me his best this-is-going-to-so-rock scrunched-up face. I remember thinking that *he* kind of looked like Satan.

"I don't know this song," I said as soon as I heard the first drumbeat.

"Give it a second to play, man," Maurice said. "You got to know this song! It's *everywhere*. B104 plays it all the time."

"I don't *listen* to rock and roll!" I countered. "I'm not allowed to. I've never listened to B104."

This was quite true; I was allowed to listen to only Christian music and only if it didn't have drums. My church said that drums harnessed evil spirits.

"You guys have never heard this song? *Are you kidding?*" asked Maurice, acting as if the two of us Christian school kids were a freak show. "This is "Pour Some Sugar on Me" by Def Leppard. This song rocks my socks off," said Maurice. "It's such a *nasty* little song."

Maurice sang the lyrics and shook his head to the beat every time the chorus came on.

"I cannot believe you have never heard this song," he continued. "Do you ever get to listen to any good music?"

That's when I asked him if he had ever heard of Amy Grant. He hadn't. I pretended like I was a big fan of hers. Of course, at the time, I was allowed to listen to only her slow stuff.

Determined, Maurice went through about ten tapes trying to find one song that he thought we might have heard. But he couldn't find one. I did tell him that I heard Michael Jackson's "Bad" on the Pepsi commercial once. He rolled his eyes.

"Wow. So you guys are pretty sheltered, huh?" he asked.

"I guess so, but we don't look at it like that. It's just who we are. We follow Jesus, and so that means we stay away from rock music."

"Are you Amish?" he asked. "'Cuz I have a friend who used to be Amish. But I guess he converted to 'heathen' when he was sixteen."

"No, we're not Amish," I replied. I was becoming less and less impressed with Maurice. But he kept asking my friend and me questions. Eventually, he began asking us about girls.

"You guys must not get much action with the ladies, huh?"

"I've held hands with a girl," said my friend.

"*What?!* That's all you've done? That's stinkin' hilarious, man. Gosh, you don't know what you're missing. By the time I was sixteen, I had seen it all."

As I listened to Maurice ask my friend a hundred questions about his experiences, I was praying that he wouldn't turn and do the same to me. The questions were personal and used words that I was allowed to use only in bathrooms and hospitals.

"So you two have never seen breasts," said Maurice with a laugh, like he already knew the answer to that question. He looked at me.

I quickly shook my head no.

Maurice laughed a big hearty laugh and then asked, "Do you want to?"

As soon as I heard those words, my heart felt like it stopped beating in my chest.

Of course, my great influence of a friend quickly said, "Sure, I'll look at them!"

"How about you, Mr. Matt? You want to see 'em?" asked Maurice again, rather forcefully.

"That's OK; I don't think I want to see the pictures," I said with all the conviction I could muster up. But really, I was curious. Inside my naive mind, a vicious game of tug-of-war began between my desire to see a woman without clothes and the preaching that I had heard since I was five. *Keep your heart pure* kept running over and over in my head. *Run as fast as you can away from temptation.* I could feel the war happening within my spirit. *Satan's like a lion, and he wants to eat you alive.* But the curiosity of seeing those pictures was killing me. *I wonder what Joseph would do … He would drop everything and run.* A nervous excitement had worked its way through my bones. My young teenage senses were on overdrive. Sure, I was saying no out loud, but inside, I was curious—*really* curious.

"Come on," said Maurice. "You know you want to see the pictures. God ain't gonna send you to hell for one little peek at some of the most beautiful breasts you will ever see."

"Matthew, it's no big deal," said my friend. "It's only some pictures."

"Yeah, man; I got them right here," said Maurice, opening his glove compartment. "Two magazines full of some very beautiful pictures of naked women doing some unbelievable things."

When I walked into school the next day, I realized that I had become quite unpopular overnight—because I had refused to look at the pictures. My friend, on the other hand, had become a star—Mr. Popularity, in fact.

While I had driven the car that day, he had sat in the backseat and thumbed through those magazines. He had stories to tell. He had pictures to describe. He had gotten an inside look at what the world looked like on the other side. By the way most of the guys treated him, you would have thought he had just matured three years in twelve hours. Honestly, a part of me kind of envied him. There were many occasions over the next few months that I wished I *had* looked at the pictures. My friend and his buddies had inside jokes about him seeing the pictures. I wasn't privy to the inside jokes. In fact, they purposefully left me out of them. And when you're in the tenth grade, is there anything more humiliating than being left out of an inside joke? At that time, I didn't think so.

My only solace from the entire situation was that my heart had been left pure. I had stayed perfect. Because I had run from temptation, I thought I had kept my heart from being contaminated. But that changed.

There was one normal teacher at my school that year. Somehow, he caught wind of the story and decided to talk with me after class one afternoon.

"I heard what happened a few weeks ago," he said, looking at me steadily.

"You did?" I asked, somewhat embarrassed that a teacher had found out about my hearing rock music and almost looking at pictures of naked women. "Yeah, well," I said, "the last few weeks have been some of the worst of my life."

"I can imagine," said my teacher.

I listened to him intently despite the fact that his bald head was reflecting a lot of light and making it hard to concentrate.

"Life is never simple when you make a decent choice, Matthew. Good choices often complicate things. People make fun. You're tempted to feel proud of yourself for making a good decision. It can be pretty rough."

"You don't think I should be proud of myself?" I asked.

"Nah, I don't think so," he said in a very pleasant voice. "In reality, you're really no better than the 'other guy.'"

"What? But I didn't look. *He looked!*"

"Yeah, I know you didn't look. But that's not what makes a heart pure. You wanted to, right?"

"Well, sure; I guess." I stopped talking for a second, and then I grinned. "Yes, I wanted to look. What guy wouldn't want to?"

"I figured," he said, obviously trying not to smile. "Matthew, always remember this ..."

My teacher looked at me like he was staring at a younger version of himself.

"You made a great choice a few weeks ago, but the opportunity for you to have made the bad choice still existed in your heart, buddy. And the fact that you've walked around here for the last month or so like you're a little better than everyone else is just as sinful as looking at those pictures. Our hearts are naturally evil. Don't think for a second that you are above that. I've made that mistake before."

My teacher's words hit me hard that day. They surprised my fifteen-year-old mind. When he stopped me after class and told me that he knew the story, I expected him to congratulate me, pat me on the back, and say, "Well done, you good and faithful servant." Instead, he put me on the same level as my friend. I know now that my teacher could have gotten into a lot of trouble for having that conversation. He knew the story, yet he didn't report it. He talked to my friend, but he didn't punish him.

On that particular day, when my teacher spoke to me, I didn't get what he was trying to say. In fact, I didn't fully understand the wisdom he was communicating about the capability of my heart until I began truly traveling with Jesus many years later.

Today, every time I get a clear picture of what my heart is capable of, I think of what that teacher shared with me many years ago. Sure, when I make a good decision my heart escapes being filled with more junk. But that action in and of itself does not make my heart pure. Relearning Jesus has taught me that my heart is capable of a lot; it's in my brokenness and humility that I see just how much. I didn't know that when I was fifteen.

Two and a half years went by before I had *another* chance to see pictures of naked women. And that time, I looked. I pretty much jumped out of my skin for the chance to see something so beautiful and decadent. But unlike my friend's experience from a couple of years before, my life didn't go from mediocre to fame and popularity overnight when I looked at pornography for the first time. When I experienced porn for the first time, I just felt a whole bunch of guilt. Guilt chased me like a lion chases a gazelle. And for much of my young adult life, I was eaten alive.

Only recently have I fully begun to understand the weight of that first encounter with pornography. Sure, when I looked at the women in those pictures that day, it sent my curiosity through the roof and gave my mind enough visual stimulant to rule my imagination for many months. But that's not all that happened.

That first encounter also created in me a false sense of security. It was a security that said to me, "If I stay away from pornography, my heart will be made good in the eyes of Jesus." So, that's what I did; well, that's what I tried to do. I poured every bit of spiritual and emotional energy into staying away from pornography.

The more I pursued trying to *feel* pure, the more I failed. And every time I failed, like clockwork, I would venture through the motions of trying to *make* Jesus deem me good again. I did that over and over and over again. Years went by (ten to be exact) before I realized my thinking was spiritually destructive. Eventually, I learned that nothing I could do would make Jesus deem me good. Only he could make my heart good, and that was not something that would happen instantly.

Sure, I can create spiritual habits that will clean up my heart or keep it from getting mucked up by sin, but I can do nothing to make God deem it good. *That's* what my teacher was trying to tell me that day—that if I depend on my own actions to make me pure, I would never see God.

I had read many times before that Jesus said a person with a pure heart sees God. And because I want to see God, probably more than any other spiritual thing, I have worked the hardest at trying to make my heart pure. I wanted to make it pure enough to see God. And not surprisingly, that battle has probably been the most complicated part of my Christian life. But because of my desire to see God, I keep walking with Jesus on the journey. And once in a while, I do get a glimpse.

Just not as often as others claim.

Pause and Reflect

What does the idea of a "pure heart" mean to you?

How do you attempt to keep your heart pure?

CONFESSION IS GOOD FOR THE EYES

People who see God—really see God—on a regular basis are sometimes intimidating to me. Their lifestyles and words rub up against mine. I don't necessarily feel judgment or guilt. At least, I don't feel that from them. It's my experience that a pure heart doesn't reflect such things as judgment or impatience. But sometimes I do have this sense of conviction and spiritual longing when I meet such a person.

I believe a pure heart is one of the most beautiful and attractive qualities I have ever witnessed in a human being. It doesn't mean people with pure hearts are perfect; it simply means they're willing to stay on the journey with Jesus for the long haul. They don't stop and make faith a destination. They know the path to a pure heart requires following Jesus every day, and they put what they know into practice.

My grandmother always taught me that a pure heart happens when a person confesses often. For ten years I watched my grandmother pray. When she turned eighty-one, she moved in with my family. She shared a bedroom with my little sister. I learned some of the most profound lessons about Jesus from watching her. When Mammom prayed, she did it the old-fashioned way—kneeling beside her bed, hands in folded position resting on the bedspread, her eyes always closed. She told me once that when she prayed at night, she'd always first ask Jesus to forgive her for all the sin that she had committed that day. When we were kids, my sister and I always found this a little humorous.

"Mammom, what sins do you confess?" I asked her one time. "You seem perfect to me."

"Oh, you'd be surprised," she said in the most innocent of tones. "Sometimes when you see me smiling and having a good attitude,

I'm only doing that on the outside to make people think I'm happy. But on the inside, I'm thinking all kinds of bad things."

"Really?" My fourteen-year-old head didn't buy it.

"Just last week, Jean told me something in confidence, and the very next day, I was on the phone with Regina telling her all about it," said my grandmother with a grin. Jean and Regina were Mammom's best friends.

My grandmother never wanted to miss a chance to see Jesus throughout her day.

"I know I forget some things," she'd say. "So, I always ask the Holy Spirit to come and help me remember. I haven't got the greatest memory, you know."

My grandmother told me several times that when her heart was clean—not necessarily empty, not perfect—only then could she see God. And she did see him, too. She didn't see his face in pictures like my coworker Angela did; Mammom saw his presence in the circumstances of her life. And her life had sometimes been quite hard. She suffered a miscarriage early in her marriage. She lost Jack, her eleven-year-old son, to a ruptured appendix. She held her family together when my grandfather went through many years of depression and grief over Jack's death. She overcame a heart attack in her seventies. But when grace compelled her to confess daily, she was certain that Jesus made her heart pure.

"Confession is the most beautiful of places that God can see our hearts," she said to me once, although I am most certain she stole that from one of the many radio preachers she would listen to in the mornings. Either way, there was always something very clean and good and pure about my Mammom.

Pause and Reflect

Do you believe confession leads to a pure heart? If so, how have you seen this in your own life?

CLEAN FACE

One of my responsibilities when I was editor of *CCM* was to occasionally meet with new bands and hear their stories about why they chose to go into music. The experience was always a little formulaic and weird for me. I knew that their record label had set up the meeting hoping I would choose them for coverage in the magazine. The bands and artists would often feel pressure to put on their best "face" and to present their best stories for me to hear. It was no doubt as uncomfortable for them as it was for me at times.

One time, I had lunch with a hardcore rock band. I was less than excited about this lunch—mainly because I was not a huge fan of hardcore rock music, but also because the magazine was on a deadline, and I needed to be working back at my office. When I arrived, I joined five guys who seemed to be trying desperately to look like hard rockers. I can't help but think that trying to look like Green Day is hard and awkward, but maybe it was just hard for me to witness a band trying too hard to play that part. It always seemed fake and rehearsed. When I sat down at the table, I tried my best not to talk too much.

So I just listened to their stories.

The two men who spoke the most were both thirty. Their stories included drugs, sex, alcohol, an attempted suicide, and time in jail.

They talked about God coming into their lives a few years back and his presence saving them and their families out of hopelessness. Their stories were dramatic and impressive from an evangelical standpoint. You could tell they had shared their stories often. They were perfectly told—almost like they were reading from a teleprompter.

But despite their stories having lots of drama, they were stories I had heard a hundred times before. I could certainly appreciate the extraordinary nature of what had occurred, but I wasn't *really* moved enough by their stories to consider them for a feature in the magazine. Two of the other band members shared short stories about being raised in Christian homes, making a few mistakes, and now being completely on fire for Jesus. Again, their stories were good, much like mine, but they didn't spark a lot of interest from an editorial standpoint, either.

However, the entire time I was listening to the stories of those four men, something about the guy down at the far end of the table intrigued me. He had dark Mongolian skin. His hair was jet black, and he wore it in dreads. His look was normal for a Christian rock band. I hadn't heard his story. In fact, only a few times during the conversation had he even spoken up. When he did, there was this unfettered innocence that flowed from him. It wasn't in his words. We had *all* been sitting there, chatting about the goodness of Jesus in our stories. But something about this guy was pure. He simply reeked of Jesus. My spiritual gut kept saying to me, *Let him tell you his story.*

But honestly, I fought it a little bit. I wasn't sure I wanted to hear what Jesus was doing in his life. I was afraid that this young man's *pure* story would somehow interfere and make my own seem worthless. I was afraid his innocence would make my story feel ugly, perverted, and trite. Being near him made me feel convicted; hearing his life story might make it worse. But Jesus wouldn't let me walk away without hearing him out.

We were getting close to the end of our time together, and the young man still hadn't said much yet. So I directed the conversation toward him.

"Dude," I said, looking at him, "are you *perfect?* There's just something about you that I can't figure out."

The guys in the band started laughing hysterically.

"No, I'm being serious," I said, trying to get the others to be quiet. "There is just something very 'Christlike,' for lack of a better term, about you. It's a spirit or something. I can't really explain …"

"Matthew," said one of the other guys in the band, still laughing, "we're laughing because he gets that everywhere we go. People *always* identify Jesus in his life."

"Well, I can see why," I said smiling, stumbling over my words a bit. "I'm sitting here feeling convicted by you. And *you* have hardly said anything."

"Tell him your story, man," coaxed the lead singer.

The young man spoke up. It wasn't as spectacular as I imagined. I guess I expected something miraculous by the way Jesus had been trying to get me to talk to him. But his story was simple, really.

His parents were people who pursued Jesus passionately and encouraged him to do the same. He hadn't gotten into any big trouble. Life just hadn't given him the opportunity to do so. He looked at me and said that he didn't really understand why people responded to him in that way. But they did, and when they did, he simply praised Jesus for the opportunity to be something of a light in a person's life.

"Matthew," said the lead singer, seemingly exasperated because his bandmate wouldn't share too much. "This man spends time with Jesus. He prays. He makes an effort to know his Savior. His life is pure. He's not perfect or anything, but Jesus blesses that boy because he is faithful at spending time with Jesus. He knows him."

I liked the fact that someone else had to tell his story. The young man, who played bass and had fascinating hair, had a story that wasn't the least bit rehearsed. He seemed to be humble, a lot more humble than I am most of the time. Thankfully, I didn't walk away from that conversation feeling perverted, but I did leave asking Jesus to give me a little taste of what that bass player had. I walked away thinking I need to readdress my own desire to really know Jesus. Knowing Jesus is of great importance to a pure heart.

GOD GETS QUIET

October 22, 1998, was a whirlwind of a day. It was on that Sunday evening when my personal relationship with Jesus hit a breaking point. I wasn't at a church service or a revival or a music concert. I was home alone, sinning.

On that evening, I had come to Jesus with yet another confession. I think I must have been known in heaven for my many confessions. I made a habit of confessing my sin. Nearly every time I fell short of God's glory—which was often—I'd offer Jesus my apology. This particular time, I was apologizing for my regular once-every-couple-of-months bout with sexual gratification through the beautiful convenience of online pornography.

Locked away in my bedroom, I had spent the better half of that Sunday afternoon diving headfirst into my own little world of sexual images. I invested three *glorious* hours into high-speed, downloadable ecstasy. I wasn't addicted to porn—at least, *I* didn't think so—but I did have a haphazardly scheduled, few-times-a-year habit. It was my little secret. It was one of many sinful habits on a list that included pride, low self-esteem, selfishness, and anger, all of which I would often try to kick cold turkey, to no avail.

My regular stint with sin always included a "fall flat on my face before God" declaration of repentance. It was always a heartfelt, beautifully executed, climaxing dismount. I had perfected the art of confessing. And this particular confession was no different. My guilt-induced Jesus whimpering began shortly after my cyberescapade ended. "Jesus, I am *so* sorry. If you forgive me one more time, I will never let this happen again," was my usual plea bargain. But I meant what I said. I truly thought it would never happen again. I hated sinning—not necessarily because of the act itself, but because of the way it made me feel afterward: *gross and unworthy—right up there with child molesters and rapists and abortionists*. One time the guilt from sin hit me so hard that I literally became nauseated and ended up vomiting in the office toilet.

God had been enduring my repulsive apology routine for years: I'd sin, I'd feel guilty, I'd fall on my face and ask for forgiveness, and—*bam*—I'd be forgiven. It worked this way every single time. In my mind, there wasn't any chance God wouldn't accept me back into his ever-loving arms. I knew that freedom and grace were a part of his character, and I made a habit of taking advantage of that.

Every single time I went to God and asked for his forgiveness, I had *always* been taken back into his arms rather quickly. Almost instantly, after saying a few quick words, I would feel comfort again. I foolishly assumed that it was his responsibility to forgive me and make me feel better. Let's face it—he's the God of grace and mercy, right? A waiting period with God is not common; it was my experience that he was quick, to the point, and *always* there.

For me, Jesus was my personal "God ATM." Every time I needed acceptance or mercy or love or grace or freedom, I would just go to the ATM and make a withdrawal. And *that* day was no different. Even though I had spent the better part of an afternoon giving in to the temptation of sin, I had no doubt that I would soon feel the warmth of his graceful presence just like many times before; he always listened to me with his merciful ear. *Always!*

However on *that* day, it was a very different story. On *that* day, God wasn't listening to my negotiating. It seemed my prayers weren't reaching heaven. I said them over and over again, but I still failed to feel at peace with my situation.

The ATM seemed to be out of order—or maybe out of funds. There were no gracious arms hugging me and patting me on the back such as I had always experienced before. No one was telling me, "It's going to be OK, Matthew." Instead of comfort, hope, and forgiveness, I felt very alone, abandoned, and caged—and I passionately hated those feelings.

My first thought was that perhaps God hadn't heard me ask him for forgiveness the first time. So I begged some more, and this time,

I said it louder—even trying to make it seem more meaningful than before. "God, I am *so sorry* for what I've been doing. *Please don't take your blessings away from me. Please forgive me.* I want to feel better. I need *you*."

Although I was rather impressed with those words and my perfect delivery style, still there was no word from Jesus. He wasn't making any effort to make me feel better. At that point, a million thoughts started running through my head. *This is it,* I realized. *He's finally fed up with my disgusting shenanigans, and he's going to unveil me as the fool that I am.* And still he was silent. He had never been silent with me before. I didn't know what to do. I hate silence. It's one thing when someone is just quiet because there's nothing to talk about, but when someone is silent *on purpose* because he or she no longer wants to partake in a conversation with you—that's a whole other story. But I believe now that we can all learn from those uncomfortable moments when God is silent.

Consider the moments in biblical history when God was silent toward his people for a long period of time. Remember Joseph and his run-in with Potiphar's wife? She made a sexual advance toward him; he refused her advance—even ran out of the bedroom. The woman became embarrassed and irritated with Joseph, so she told her husband that Joseph had tried to force himself on *her.* Poor Joseph ended up spending fourteen years in prison for a crime he never committed. And God remained silent in Joseph's situation. Only a few times did Joseph get a glimpse of hope that he would one day be free. But for the better part of fourteen excruciating years, God seemed to be absent in Joseph's life. When God is silent, it's easy to get frustrated and angry over his apparent lack of interest in what is going on in your particular life situation.

I Had to Stop Running

I've heard many pastors, teachers, writers, singers, small-group leaders, and regular people say a lot of *stuff* about what it means to have a pure heart. Most of them concentrate a lot of time on sexual purity. We Christians use words like *abstain* and *resist* and *run* when talking about sexual temptation. We use the words a lot.

I have grown tired of hearing these words as they relate to purity. It's not that I believe these actions of running and resisting aren't practical ways to avoid getting into "sexual" trouble once in a while. But honestly, resisting, abstaining, and running have never worked for me. Maybe I have the wrong kind of shoes or something. Maybe I don't have the right equipment to abstain. But I guess I've listened to an awful lot of men and women tell me that running hasn't worked very well for them, either. I wish it did work. I wish the temptation to sin could be outrun. It would make my spiritual life a bit simpler, I believe.

While relearning Jesus, I've learned that in order for my heart to be pure, whether from lust or pride or fear or unkindness or whatever I personally war against, it takes something very different from running and resisting. In fact, I learned the hard way that I can't run fast enough to keep my heart pure and escape sin. I'd constantly be running and getting absolutely nowhere. I used to run all the time. Sometimes I'm still tempted to run today. It's a part of my spiritual DNA to run. It's programmed inside of me somewhere.

I know and have spoken to so many people who are running

now. When they tell me their stories, I see the look of frustration and tiredness in their eyes. Some of them are afraid to say their sin out loud. They give it to me in code. They're afraid I might judge them or think less of them because they just admitted to me that they're addicted to pornography or unemotional sexual hookups or over-the-counter drugs or whatever else we humans get ourselves into. I know that feeling of fear, of saying it out loud. I've spoken to others in code before too.

Every one of these people asks me if I know a secret. They hope I have some kind of an answer that they haven't learned yet. They're looking for an easy way (or just any way) out of their sin. They're looking to be suddenly fixed; they keep praying and hoping that Jesus will come into their lives and miraculously remove the temptation from their lives. I know that look in their eyes because I've lived it. I still live it at times.

For me, it was almost as if temptation and I would play a game. As soon as I saw the temptation coming from a long way off, I'd put on my jogging shoes. I'd run as fast as I could. I'd say Bible verses. I'd take cold showers. I'd do push-ups. I'd think about butterflies. I'd call my accountability partner. I'd do anything to try to outrun temptation. And once in a while, I'd win a match or a race. And that would feel really good. But most of the time, temptation would outrun me and then I'd lose. I'd lose because I was depending on my own ability, *thinking* I was depending on the power of Jesus in my life.

Sure, I've met men who are recovering sex addicts who wish they had run. In fact, one actually told me to "just run, man. You'll eventually find enough strength to run faster than temptation. It just happens, I promise."

And I've met women living in the aftermath of marriages destroyed by affairs who wish they or their husbands had resisted. The situations are devastating. And so many have a battle strategy or a game plan, and I have tried them. The methods I've heard work for a while, but then it comes back on a day that I am tired or weak or frail (which is every day of my life, practically). And I lose—again.

But most of the time running and resisting don't work. I was devastated when I learned that my acts of resistance wouldn't (and couldn't) make my heart pure. It left me feeling empty and insecure in my faith.

I so wish I had a secret to share.

Only my time with Jesus has made purity of heart even an option for me. Traveling with Jesus on this journey continues to introduce me to the grace and forgiveness and purity that his blood supplies. When I finally decided to fall down and let Jesus pick me up, I began to slowly feel the nature of what grace is supposed to do to a person like me. And after falling down more than a few times and letting Jesus continue to pick me back up out of my filth, I stopped running. I learned to accept his grace as a gift again and again. The gift is often hard to accept, I do admit.

Suddenly, it dawned on me that I had been running nonstop for years. I tried outrunning lust. I tried outrunning bitterness. I tried outrunning pride. I tried outrunning fear. Everything my heart collected over the years, I tried to outrun. Basically, if it was a problem in my life, I just got prepared for a good game of tag. My problems would always return and say, "Tag, you're it."

Jesus has taught me to fall down a lot. Falling down and humbling myself in front of Jesus is usually when I see him. It's when my heart is at its purest—not perfect, but just clean from confession and a little bit of humility. I still sometimes see things that my eyes shouldn't see. And I still hear things that my ears shouldn't hear. And sometimes I do things that I don't want to do.

But it's my sincere desire to be completely dependent on Jesus. I want my life to hardly be able to function on its own. Jesus has to remind me that my actions are selfish, that I'm completely useless without him on the journey. That's why I don't have a secret to share. If I did, then that would mean I had *arrived* somewhere. And you might be tempted to look for that place, too.

Today, when I feel the effects of temptation, when I can sense it coming toward me, Jesus tells me not to run. He tells me to just fall down and resist depending on my own ability. And when I do, sometimes when I finally stand up again, I have just enough strength to say no to whatever it is that is ailing me.

As you can imagine, I fall down on my face a lot.

But I've learned that purity comes through humility. Purity can be seen over the horizon when my friend Daniel calls me up and asks me how I'm doing—*really* doing. Purity gives me a chance when I am weak enough to be completely honest with my friend. Purity comes when I know that this story I am living is not about me—when I live out the truth that my story is about being a part of Jesus' story.

I don't expect perfection anymore, but I do anticipate grace. I know that grace must be my lifeblood. Grace must be the thing that keeps me from running on my own strength. I get a glimpse of God when I simply follow Jesus as he leads me to invest my life into other people and not into myself.

Now, I wake up most mornings desiring to see God do something through me or in front of me or despite me. I want that to be the desire of my heart. With that being my constant prayer, I know I cannot journey alone.

Pause and Reflect

What sin keeps you from that pure heart you've always dreamed about?

For me, it's about dependency, but what is purity of heart all about for you?

HAPPY TO SEE YOU

Nicaragua in January is hot and muggy, much like a Houston summer. When we (a team of about twenty people) arrived at the airport in Managua in January 2003, there were two large white vans there to pick us up and take us to the hotel.

I stared out the window in disbelief most of the way to our hotel. As we drove down the mostly dirt streets, we couldn't help but be physically and emotionally moved by the desperation and poverty that consumed the city. Everywhere I looked, I saw poor faces—hopeless, alone, fearful, dirty. The people looked like they had been locked up inside the jail of reality, and they couldn't find the key. In fact, most of them looked as if they had stopped searching. Their faces screamed, *We have no way of getting out!*

I was in Nicaragua with a large child relief organization. Upon arrival, I knew that there would be a chance that I would be able to meet the child my wife and I sponsor. Three days later, I was told that Carlos would be at one of the camps that we would be visiting.

When I met eight-year-old Carlos, he was singing Jesus songs in his one-room schoolhouse with about seventy-five other poor children and a dedicated group of adult leaders. As we got out of the van, we could hear the children's praise spilling out into the very poor streets. One of the women who was with us, a thirtysomething singer, looked at me upon hearing the sweet sound of music. "Do you hear that?" she asked. "That is one of the most beautiful sounds I have ever heard." She was right. The sound was about as close to magical as I had ever encountered. When I first heard the sounds of those young Spanish-speaking voices singing out loud and their little hands clapping cheerfully, I couldn't believe my ears.

While the others continued to sing and clap, Carlos joined me out in the common area of the children's church and school. Their building was surrounded by some of the poorest neighborhoods I have witnessed. It appeared to be desolate for so many.

Carlos was quite tall for his age. His deep brown hair was sloppy and looked as if it hadn't been washed in a few days. He smelled of chocolate, thanks to a snack the children had just eaten. We chatted through an interpreter. Knowing that Carlos was only eight years old, I did my best to make my questions short, simple, and to the point. One of his answers to my silly questions left me speechless.

"Is there anything that you want, Carlos?" I asked, looking directly into his large brown eyes. "Is there anything, anything at all, that you *really* want?"

I watched as Carlos glanced at his interpreter and then listened intently to him as he translated my words. Carlos looked at me and shook his head.

"*Nada,*" he said to the interpreter. *Nada* is one of the few words in Spanish that I actually know.

"Are you sure?" I asked again. "Do you want a TV? A soccer ball? Toys? Anything at all?

Again, Carlos looked up at his interpreter and then responded again, "*No, nada.*"

I asked the same question one more time, thinking to myself that there must be at least one selfish dream that this kid might have. This time Carlos thought about it for a moment. He turned to the interpreter and said shyly, *"¿Puedo tener una cama a dormir?"*

"He wants a bed to sleep on," said the interpreter.

He doesn't have a bed? He's poor enough to not have a bed, yet too shy and quiet and content to ask for one? And he refused to ask for anything remotely selfish?

I was speechless.

As I sat there and talked with Carlos, I couldn't help but be amazed at this kid's heart. He was happy. Even though he did not have a bed, it took him forever to think of something that he needed *or even wanted.* Despite his surroundings being so ugly and poor and, to an American like me, very much hopeless, Carlos and the other children and their noble leaders found reason and energy to praise Jesus.

I saw a vivid picture of Jesus that day on the face of Carlos and on the faces of the other children. That night my heart was perplexed. I couldn't sleep. So, I walked around inside the comfort of the beautiful five-star hotel where I was staying, and I prayed this prayer:

Jesus, I feel guilty for seeing you in this moment, when it seems so gross and poor and poverty-stricken here. I feel like a stupid, proud American to even think about seeing you in such a place. It seems so very cliché. But the kids' hearts that I witnessed today are so pure that they seem to be able to see you and praise you despite their circumstances. I believe with all of my heart that they see you. Would you please give me the freedom and purity to see you too? I want that.

Jesus showed up on several occasions over the next few days. I didn't make a big deal about it to the others when I saw him. I didn't jump up and down with excitement; I didn't have the energy, nor did I feel the need to point him out to everyone around. In all honesty, I was just happy I was able to see him.

Pause and Reflect

In what ways do you see God? What happened the last time you did?

How does having a pure heart help you see God?

I have always found that mercy bears richer fruits than strict justice.

—Abraham Lincoln

Blessed are the merciful, for they will be shown mercy. (Matt. 5:7 NIV)

—Jesus

THE HARD THING ABOUT MERCY

My friend Lisa was driving to meet with a troubled teen from her youth group. On the ride over, she decided to call me for some much-needed encouragement.

As long as I have known Lisa, she has always put a great deal of effort into spending time with kids. But it's not just time she spends. She works hard at investing in the spiritual and emotional lives of the young girls in her youth ministry. She has seen a lot of sad things happen in her ministry time. If there is anyone in the world I know who understands the concept that showing mercy often hurts like hell, it's her. She's learned this the hard way—by showing a lot of mercy.

"Hey, Mateo!" Lisa always found the need to call me by the Spanish equivalent of my name. I'm still not sure why. "Well, I'm on my way over to the juvenile detention center," she said in a sarcastic, singsong tone. *"Again!"*

"Which one of your kids has been sent there?" I asked.

"I probably shouldn't say," she replied. "You probably don't know her. This girl has stolen her parents' car two or three time since I've known her. And this is the first time her parents have actually allowed the police to arrest her. On top of that, she's tried to commit suicide before, and she's anorexic. Lucky me, huh?"

"*Wow.* I'm sorry to hear this," I said. "How *old* is she, Lisa?"

"She's fourteen," she said, softly. "And the thing is, Mateo, I have run out of things to say to this girl. I have spent I don't know how many hours of my youth ministry investing into her life … and you know me; I don't mind troubled kids. In fact, I *love* them. But I don't know what else to do for her. I feel helpless. So, I called you for some Mateo support!"

"Has she ever improved?"

"Oh yeah, she does great for about two months. And then falls hard—and usually it's so much harder than before. She's probably going to get sent away to a girls' home. I'm scared for her, you know? I don't know if she will make it there."

"I don't know what to say, Lisa."

"I don't expect to hear any magic words."

"I know it's hard to give and give and give when nothing ever seem to change," I said. "That's the crazy thing about ministry, I guess; the 'return on investment' is not *really* the point. It's the fact that Jesus has asked us to give and give and give without expecting anything in return. I don't believe the lack of change should change our willingness to extend mercy."

"I know," said Lisa. "I just want this girl to see the dream that God has for her, that's all. It *really* is hard to keep giving and giving and not see at least that. Do you know that I have been hanging out with her for more than a year and a half? And now, we're right back at the beginning."

"I actually doubt that's true, Lisa. This girl's circumstance may seem like she's back at the beginning, but she's probably not. I have little doubt that one of these days she'll look back on all of this and remember you."

"I'm not so sure," said Lisa, laughing.

"Oh, I think you'll be surprised. I think she'll one day look back on all of this time you've invested, and she'll see her need to make some changes."

"If she lives that long," said Lisa with a hint of seriousness in her voice. "Anyway, I am just emotionally wiped out from all of this. Would you please pray for me? I covet your prayers. It's just going to be hard to see her in jail."

Mercy is indeed hard. Every time I have seen the ongoing presence of mercy and compassion, there's always a point when the person doing the giving gets burned out. It's almost inevitable, I think. The act itself—the emotional, spiritual, and physical investment—is sometimes just tiring. At times in my life when I'm brave enough to show mercy, there are moments when it feels like I've reached a dead end. Everything inside says to give up, but that's hard too, because mercy creates a bond. The connection that Jesus forms between the giver and the recipient cannot simply be forgotten. And let me be truthful. Too often I begin my ventures into showing mercy with an end—a good end—in mind. Whether it's for the recipient or me, I usually expect something miraculous to happen. And when it doesn't turn out like I had prayed and hoped and imagined, discouragement often abounds. Jesus must have figured that if he had let me in on how hard it is to show mercy and compassion without return, I would resist giving with all of my heart.

I once had the pleasure of hearing a wise man say this: To show mercy *once* is expected. To show mercy a *thousand times* is generous. To show mercy for a *lifetime* is to be the Savior of the world. So, let's always be generous.

I didn't always understand my part in mercy. I was once a bit stingy and selfish in my compassion and forgiveness. Sure, I gave of myself and my money when the moment was convenient. But the concept of mercy being a part of who I am as a person was quite foreign to me, which is not surprising considering I knew a lot more about the absence of mercy than I did about showing it.

Pause and Reflect

What does mercy mean to you?

Do you have a memorable experience when somebody showed you mercy?

What's your biggest challenge in regard to living a life of mercy?

DON'T WAIT TOO LONG TO SHOW MERCY

I've written about Devon before (in my book *The Coffeehouse Gospel*). He's a man whose story I read many years ago online in one of those diary-type Web sites. His story was a sad portrayal of where sin can leave an individual. Devon was a twenty-six-year-old troubled soul working as a male prostitute in the downtown business district of Miami. He made nearly $3,000 a week "servicing" high-profile businessmen and women whom he met in chat rooms online.

It had been his goal to escape his illegal employment by moving away from his hometown of Washington DC to the southeast coast of Florida. He hoped to make a new start, but a drug habit and the need to make some quick cash lured him back into his controversial trade.

Devon's story included big, fancy parties where he was paid top dollar to "perform," interactions with C- and D-level celebrities who would buy him nice clothes and good cocaine, and the occasional meetings with politicians who paid mostly for his willingness to keep quiet. After almost two years of living this life, Devon became depressed and suicidal, and he started seeking support.

Devon visited a church in South Florida, hoping to find a life that was real and authentic. He liked the church. He ended up joining a Bible study, and six months into his time at this church, he broke down in front of the group of six men and shared his story. Two of the men were completely freaked out by the details of Devon's life. They refused to be a part of a Bible study with someone of his background. The pastor of the church tried to intervene, but news of Devon's story traveled quickly around the church. Feeling even more defeated, Devon left the church.

Unfortunately, nearly two years after visiting that church, Devon ended his life tragically in an apparent suicide. No one knows for sure, but it seems unlikely that he ever found the love he was looking for. At least, he didn't find it in this lifetime.

Stories like Devon's can be found all across the world and in nearly every type of community. People whose lives are devastated by sin, confusion, and hopelessness end up turning to the church for acceptance and love, but instead they find judgment, fear, and resistance. I've seen this behavior firsthand over and over again in the churches I have visited. This is why I am thoroughly convinced that individuals with a desire to follow Jesus must learn to love—with no strings attached.

Mercy Shouldn't Have Stipulations

As clumsy as showing mercy feels sometimes, I always believe in it.

James was prone to making stupid mistakes. He made a lot of them. If it wasn't his sleeping around (or trying to) that got him into trouble, it was driving ninety-five in a forty, underage drinking, and hanging out with a crowd that did all of the above and then some. Unfortunately for him, James had the luck of post-1992 Michael Jackson. Except, if James were caught with his pants down (and one time that actually happened), punishment usually followed.

When I moved to northern Virginia, seventeen-year-old James began working for me at the coffeehouse/live-music venue I managed. Over time, we developed the kind of relationship that allowed me to be the one "adult" he would sometimes listen to. As I got to know James, he began to open up more. We developed a great deal of trust between us. Because our religious pasts were similar, I chose not to "preach" at him *too* much. Rather than harping on him about his smoking and drinking habits, I chose to make sure that he felt mercy from at least one individual in his life. But over those two years of working alongside James, I wondered a million times if I was doing the right thing—because it was one of the hardest things I have ever been able to do.

One night, about an hour before James' midnight shift was to be over, he and two of his buddies were out behind the coffeehouse. With two bags of trash in my hand, I walked out the back door toward the Dumpster only to find James and his crew smoking marijuana. He was holding a partly empty bottle of vodka. Upon seeing this, I cursed and dropped the trash bags.

"Please, get inside, James!" I said, remaining as controlled as I possibly could.

As soon as those words bellowed out of my mouth, my mind began to race: *This is the third time he's done something like this. Do I call his parents this time? Do I ruin the trust that we have built? Do I tell him the same stuff he's heard a million times? How does mercy fit into all of this?*

Once the back door slammed behind us, James spoke first.

"I am so sorry that I'm putting you in another predicament you don't want to be in, Matthew," he said. "I won't let this happen again."

"You've done this before," I said, still trying to figure out what I was going to do.

"I know, bro. I am so sorry."

"I'm sure you are, James," I said with a humorless laugh. "I'd feel sorry, too, if I was a seventeen-year-old who had just gotten caught smoking pot and hitting shots at work—*again.*"

"What are you going to do?" he asked.

I didn't answer his question.

"You *promised* the last time that you would *never* put me in this position again," I said. "I *hate* this, James. This just isn't fair."

"I know," he whispered.

Two minutes went by without either of us saying a word to the other. I prayed inside my head. I'm quite sure James was praying, too. My words broke the silence.

"Get out of here, bro," I said.

When he heard those words, James' face went from desperate to confused.

"As long as you're OK to drive, then get out of here," I said.

"That's it? No lecture? You're not going to at least give me the same talk you did the last time?"

"No, I'm not," I said. "It just dawned on me, James, that I've shown you *my* mercy the last two times: I let you go but then made you promise me that you'd never do it again. But I'm realizing that's kind of like showing mercy and then attaching a bomb to it."

James stared at me intently.

"The kind of mercy Jesus shows is limitless. It doesn't come with stipulations. And besides, I don't want you promising me something you can't deliver. You don't have to promise me anything, James. I forgive you. This little event will stay between you and me. Now, get out of here. You've got to work tomorrow morning."

"Are you sure?"

"Yes, I'm sure. Go."

"Thanks, Matthew," he said, "I promise …"

"*Don't do it*, James. Don't promise something you aren't able to keep. Just accept the gift."

James gathered his stuff and headed for the door. As he walked away, I thought of so many things that I wanted to say. I wanted to remind him that drug abuse has consequences that might not be nearly as merciful. I wanted to tell him not to forget this moment, to remember it when he was feeling like mercy didn't exist. I wanted to tell him not to take mercy for granted, but then I thought of how many times I had taken it for granted. So, as James said good-bye one last time before heading out the front door, I wanted to say a lot of things, but I kept my mouth closed—for once.

Nearly five years later, out of the blue, I got an e-mail from James. He had just started going back to church. Just two years before, he had gotten busted for possession, but a good lawyer got him out of it. Obviously, he later learned that drugs have *some* consequences. In his e-mail he also wrote, "I just wanted to thank you for showing me a kind side of Jesus; I had never met that side of him before. I'm back in church exploring my faith again."

I've shared that story only once in front of an audience. After I finished my talk, several people came up to me and said that they thought my decision not to report him was atrocious. When I asked them why, they said things like, "You could have kept him from getting arrested. He might not have ever done drugs again. Mercy could have come in the form of his parents getting involved." They were right; mercy could have come in all of those forms. But at the time I made that decision, I didn't care about the pot. I didn't care about the vodka. I was more concerned about him experiencing a small—*very small*—taste of mercy, forgiveness, and grace.

Pause and Reflect

Does your mercy have limits, guidelines, or boundaries? And if so, should it?

SHOCK

If the mercy of Jesus is shocking, why shouldn't the mercy we show to others be shocking, too? Jesus' mercy *doesn't make sense*. It's alarming and peculiar. It gives and gives and gives without expecting anything from me in return. The mercy of Jesus catches me off guard at times. And I believe that's the kind of mercy that's most effective in this world—the kind that leaves me standing back and wondering what just happened. That's the kind of mercy that changes people's lives. That's the kind of mercy I need in my own life—the kind of mercy that leaves me amazed and in disbelief.

Jesus talked about mercy like this: The one who shows mercy is happy because he is shown mercy. The times in my life that I have been shown mercy are memorable, peaceful, and spiritual. It's like being reintroduced to Jesus all over again. Mercy makes me think to myself, *Ah, this is what following Jesus is supposed to feel like.*

But revealing that kind of mercy takes a selfless person. I know exactly what mercy looks like, and still I fail to show it often enough. Sure, it's pretty simple for me to show mercy in a situation like James'. It's just me showing forgiveness. It hardly takes any action at all. Certainly that kind of mercy isn't *always* easy, but in many cases it is indeed easy.

For me, the hard-to-show mercy is the intentional kind of mercy that I am called to hand out daily and willingly in the lives of those in need, in want, or in pain. That kind of mercy actually takes time, effort, energy, and finances on my part. On the journey, Jesus has really been teaching me that he simply wants mercy to be a part of my lifestyle—in that it becomes natural, perhaps even an obsession, for me to give of myself freely and openly in someone's life.

In the past, I thought I lived this way. I've fed the homeless on Thanksgiving and New Year's Day. I support a child with Compassion International and one with World Vision. I give money when disasters hit. I put coins in the red Salvation Army kettles at Christmas. I give my leftover clothes and household items to people in need. But does any of this really cost me all that much? And isn't mercy something that is free but costs a lot?

My friend Eileen believes so. She believes it with all of her heart.

A Conversation with Eileen

I shared part of Eileen's story in another book. She was the brave woman who forged past the skepticism and negativity of close-minded Christian men and finally got to Jerusalem as a missionary. Today, Eileen lives in a two-room flat on the east side of the Holy City. She works with Hebrew youth and young adults. Her work has helped develop Jesus-centered mission camps all over Israel. In the winter, she translates Christian literature into Hebrew. However, before all of that, Eileen learned from her mother and father how to celebrate Jesus through mercy.

"People have always raised their eyebrows at what my family and I have done," writes Eileen. "I stopped long ago caring what others think. I'm not serving them. Mercy knows no boundaries in my opinion."

Eileen's stories and rousing spirit often left me feeling affected in my faith. I wanted Eileen's passion about mercy to be shared. So, I asked her a few questions about Jesus, mercy, and receiving mercy. Some of her answers are a little out of the ordinary. But shouldn't I have expected as much from a fifty-eight-year-old woman who enjoys a little tequila with her vanilla ice cream?

Matthew: Eileen, what is your first memory of feeling mercy?

Eileen: My mother was full of compassion, love, and mercy. As you know, I grew up in a small town in the southern part of Alabama. That little town was 50 percent white and 50 percent black. And very much divided. My family had very little growing up, but that didn't stop my mom from giving. When I was four years old, we would get up very early in the morning on Mondays, Wednesdays, and Fridays. We drove about fifteen miles to the other side of the town, and we'd deliver fruits, vegetables, breads, and canned goods to the poor people. We had a big garden, and that was my mom's way of giving back. Mom would often help them with their finances, balance their checkbooks, and even give them tips on raising children. Those have to be my earliest memories. Even though I wasn't the recipient of the mercy, I certainly felt it.

Matthew: Your mom became quite a controversy at times in your little town, didn't she?

Eileen: (Laughs.) That's an understatement. My mom caused quite a stir. The town we lived in was still very racist back then. Many of the folks Mom helped—not all, but most—were people of color. Lots of people, even the church people, didn't like that my mom associated herself with black people. We'd get letters in the mail calling my mom and dad "n—— lovers." It was scary at times. But my mom never let that influence what she did. She certainly feared for my safety a couple of times, but then she'd pray the protection of Jesus over me and move on.

Matthew: What did your father think about all of this?

Eileen: Well, Daddy was a giver in his own right. On Saturdays, he'd convert our garage into a place where poor people could come and get their cars worked on. Nearly *every* Saturday from nine to three, Daddy would work on cars. That caused more of a controversy than Mom's good deeds, because that meant black people were coming over to the "white" side of town. I remember one occasion when I was about eight or nine, Daddy saw a man pull into our driveway. He knew he had come to cause trouble. Daddy yelled, "Leeny,"—that's what he called me—"get in the house, girl." I ran into the house and then watched the scene from my bedroom window. The man was drunk and cursing and screaming, calling my dad all sorts of names, but Dad was just as patient with him as he was with the poor people. He didn't see any difference. He used to say that people like that were "needy," too. "Just needy in a different way."

Matthew: Where do you believe your parents got this innate desire to give of their lives?

Eileen: It was certainly a product of their faith. But it wasn't a faith they found at church on Sunday. It was the faith in Jesus they had learned from living life. Each of them found Jesus' words about the poor and needy and sick to be *real*. So, instead of making lots of money, they really concentrated on investing it into people. I always laugh when I think about this, but I pretty much watched most of my inheritance get given away to people every day of my life. And I think about that now and am blown away by how special a gift that was to me.

Matthew: How did your mom and dad's way of life influence your own life?

Eileen: I think when you have parents like I had, you can either run far away from that kind of lifestyle or you embrace it fully. I know people who grew up in homes like mine, and those people are now extremely bitter about what their parents put them through—the ridicule and all. But I embraced it. I got teased a little when I was in high school, but it wasn't about my hair or my clothes or my weight—it was because my parents were being nice to people. How can I really be upset about that? My parents walked the narrow road. They taught me what it meant to be the salt of the earth. And surprise, surprise, Matthew! It had nothing to do with being at church every Sunday or singing good songs or reading the right books. It had nothing to do with Bible studies and choir practice and Sunday school. It had nothing to do with sermons and all the other stuff Christians find so much delight in. It's about giving my life away for nothing in return.

Matthew: You bring up an interesting point. I think a lot of people show mercy to get something back. What are your thoughts about that?

Eileen: It's preposterous to look at mercy as a way of *investing*.

Matthew: Oh, really? Why is that a bad term?

Eileen: It's not a *bad* term necessarily. But the word *investing* implies that you're going to get something back for what you do. It implies that when you show mercy and compassion and forgiveness, you're looking for the recipient to all of a sudden be financially stable like you. Or smart like you. Or not on drugs like you. Or hope filled like you. Showing mercy is not about the *return*, Matthew. It's about us giving—giving freely, often, and now. My parents once in a while saw some of the people who they helped get to a place where they didn't need help any longer. I've seen that in my work too. But if you're walking into a mercy experience and you're expecting your *investment* to turn a life around or make a poor person's life immaculate and perfect, you're showing mercy for the wrong reason. The *only* thing we should expect from showing mercy *is to be shown mercy*. Does mercy change lives? Yes! All the time. But if you expect it, you're going to get discouraged. You're going to get burned out. You're going to feel overwhelmed. Jesus just said give. He didn't put any stipulations on it. That wasn't his message.

Matthew: So, for you, what has been the most rewarding part of pursuing a life of mercy?

Eileen: There have been so many reasons. It's hard to say just one. I'll tell you this story: About a year and a half ago, I was here in Jerusalem, working at one of the Christian camps about an hour south of the city. I met a twelve-year-old girl named Sara. She had been rescued out of sexual slavery. Nobody knew where this little girl lived. Nobody knew her history. The pain that she had experienced had caused her to go silent; she wasn't talking at all. To look at her sad face made my heart break. She was sent to the camp because the local police knew I had a little background in sexual abuse counseling. That is a miraculous story all its own, but *I knew* Jesus had sent this little girl to the camp because he loved her. I ended up letting her live with me (again, another miracle that is hardly ever allowed).

Over the course of the next few months, I basically kept her around me the entire time. I fed her. I let her sleep in my bed while I slept on the couch. I let her come to work with me. I tried to show her love. My mission board got her medical help. Two and a half months went by, and she was still not talking. One night, we were both at home. She was coloring. I was watching TV. Out of nowhere came this little voice: "Eileen." I didn't make a big deal about it. I answered her like we spoke to each other all of the time. But inside, I was *dancing*. "Do you think God loves me?" She *asked* me that question. I was thinking, *Thank you, Jesus!* We talked for three hours. We talked about her mom and dad, who we eventually were able to locate. We talked about her faith. We talked about what had happened to her.

Now fast-forward this story by about nine months. She's home. She's getting the counseling she needs. She's rediscovering life again. I, on the other hand, am feeling depressed, alone, and very much in a spot where I didn't think I could go on in ministry. I prayed to God, *Please, show me your vision for me. I just need to know you're alive.* Matthew, that's all I prayed. About fifteen minutes later, the phone rang. It was Sara. She just called to talk to me. We had only spoken once since her return home, and that was a week after she had left my home. I thought it would be good for her to get back to a normal routine and life. But when I heard her voice on the phone that night, I knew immediately that it was God giving me a taste of his mercy. It was him reminding me of his vision for me.

Matthew: One more question: Why do you believe we struggle to show mercy the way Jesus intended?

Eileen: I think it's simple and complicated all at the same time. We *think* we're sold out for Jesus. I hear people tell me that all the time. But really, Matthew, do we even know what that means anymore? To some that means going to every church thing possible. And that's fine. But is that really the mission of Jesus—for us to be gathered around each other reading our Bibles like good little Christians? *Most of us know what Scripture teaches.* Go out and *live* it. I have a friend who lives in Maryland who twice a week gets up in the morning and drives elderly people to their doctor's appointments. I know a man in Sacramento who has a full-time job as a lawyer but manages to volunteer *twenty* hours a week at a kids' hospital. *That's* being sold out for Jesus—even though my friends would probably never use that terminology. Our priorities are screwed up, Matthew. We've got our eyes on the wrong things. We wouldn't know mercy if it bit us in the backside. I give full-time because that is what I am called to do. *Everybody* can't do that. But everybody can look for some way to *invest* in the lives of people. Mercy is needed *everywhere.*

Pause and Reflect

How is Jesus' mercy shocking to you?

Do you think the mercy that you show other people is "shocking"?

RELEARNING JESUS, RELEARNING MERCY

Valerie, a friend of mine in Nashville, is very honest about life. Raised in a Christian home since birth, she has seen a lot of the ins and outs of the conservative Christian faith. Her story isn't necessarily a new one—she's simply one of thousands, perhaps millions, of Christians who are somewhat disillusioned by their spiritual past.

Consequently, Valerie seeks more out of life than simply what the church often preaches. She admits to being bitter at times, even cynical. She's worked in Christian entertainment for many years. In her work, Valerie's had a bird's-eye view of what seemingly is wrong with pop-cultural Christianity. Of course, Valerie acknowledges the good, too, but that's sometimes harder for her to see. The politics and business of all-things Christian can dim the "light" for her a bit.

I find Valerie's friendship to be like that of a circus in the midst of ten funerals. She's lively and humorous. Her cynicism is sometimes simply delightful. Sure, she surprises me with some of the things that come out of her mouth. "I *hate* praise and worship music," she told me once with utter sarcasm. I thought, *Can you be a Christian and hate "Here I Am to Worship"?*

At the same time, Valerie also surprises me with some of the things that come out of her life, too. Her mercy toward others challenges me. The way she lives life, for me, has been quite convicting. It's shocking; the kind of relentless mercy she shows leaves those much more rigid and defined in their faith scratching their heads and questioning their intentions. But that would only happen if they knew the *real* Valerie—the nonprofessional side of her that doesn't get broadcast to everyone around. She keeps it quiet, except to her closest friends.

Everything about Valerie is big. Her personality. Her stories. Even, at times, her hair can take on a rather larger-than-life existence. Valerie and I have lunch once a month. My wife jokes about her being "the other woman" in my life. Every time Valerie and I get together, she leaves me wanting to be a little more like Jesus (and, of course, she also provides a little comic relief). At one lunch last year, she told me about something new going on in her life.

"So, have I told you what's going on in my life of late?" she asked loudly as soon as we sat down.

"No, I guess not," I replied. I was expecting to hear a story about her work or kids.

"I am *donating* my bone marrow," she said, with a hilarious look that basically said *I had no idea what I was getting myself into.*

"You're what?!" I said, completely shocked. "Does someone in your family have cancer?

"Nope. Not like that at all. I was just thinking one day that I have all of this perfectly good bone marrow in my body; why not share it? So, I put myself on the list."

I laughed.

"Wow. Valerie, that *is* brave. Will it hurt?"

"Yep, like a muthaaa."

"So, when do you go through with it?"

"That's the thing; I signed up for this *months* ago. Out of the blue, they called me last week. It could not have come at a worse time. But what are you going to do, say no to a man who is dying of cancer? So, I cleared my schedule … going into surgery next week."

"That's unbelievable; I'm proud of you."

"Why? I would hope someone would do the same thing for me," said Valerie. "But I got to tell you, it's much more of a process than I expected. I have to have blood exams; I'm going to be out of work for a while. It's *huge*."

"Do you get to meet the person you're donating to?"

"No. I don't know him. He doesn't know me. It will stay that way."

"That's crazy, Valerie. I'm excited for you. At least, I think I am."

Actually, I shouldn't have been surprised. Valerie does this kind of stuff all the time. She regularly volunteers her time to rock crying AIDS babies at a local hospital. She takes her daughters and their friends on surprise weekend getaways. She was one of the first people in line when a church bus headed south to Mississippi to help clean up after Hurricane Katrina. She has opened her home to strangers. She helps her friends when they are in need. Her life makes me feel stupid and selfish.

So what if she stands outside of the church on Sunday mornings until the praise and worship music is over? Who cares? She gives away a lot more worship to Jesus through how she lives than I do when I'm singing for thirteen minutes with my arms half-raised on Sunday morning.

I am learning mercy. When someone does me wrong and asks for forgiveness, I try to be quick to comply. But when it comes to offering mercy to strangers who do not ask, I am still in the process of letting mercy be a part of who I am.

Over these many years of being Christian, I have often asked Jesus for mercy.

I've also asked him many times where I can show mercy.

It's in his answer to that second question that I find my answer to the first.

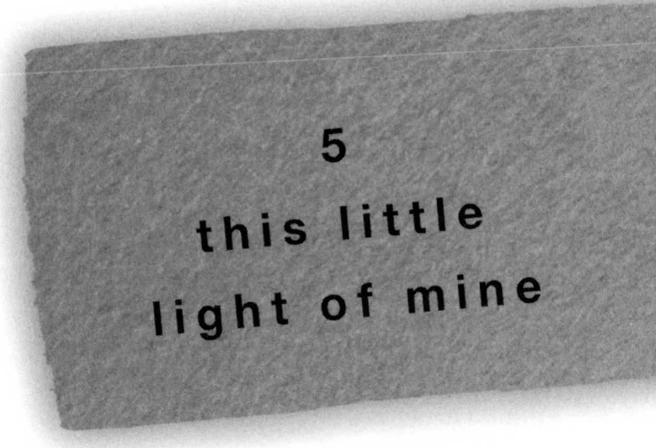

As far as we can discern, the sole purpose of human existence is to kindle a light in the darkness of mere being.

—Carl Jung, Swiss psychiatrist

You are the light of the world. (Matt. 5:14 NIV*)*

—Jesus

BLINDED BY THE LIGHT

"Daniel, I got stopped by a cop this morning," I said casually as I dropped three packets of Equal into my unsweetened iced tea. I hate Equal, actually. But I like my iced tea sweet. That's one of the few reasons I like living in the South: sugar-drenched tea. *Mmm.*

"I was driving down on Highway 123 in McLean," I continued. "He pulled me over. Gosh, I was mad."

My good friend Daniel was only half-paying attention to my story; he was much more interested in the menu. He and I had just finished working at our church's youth group where he was the church's student ministry director; I was simply a volunteer. After our gig, we would usually grab a bite at Outback. Because he had spent nearly a year in Australia, Daniel had an undying affection for anything remotely "Down Under."

"Why did the cop stop you?" Daniel finally asked. "By the way, I think I'm getting the Chicken on the Barbie."

"OK, I think I'm getting the Outback Special." Whenever my mind wasn't on food, I would almost always get the special—no thinking required. And for someone who is constantly haunted by lurking ADHD, no thinking is always a good thing.

"So, why did the cop *stop* you?" asked Daniel again, getting somewhat impatient.

"He said I was going forty-five in a thirty. But I could have sworn that I had just looked at the speedometer, and I was going thirty-seven. He said forty-five and then gave me a seventy-five-dollar ticket."

"Wow. That stinks," said Daniel somewhat sarcastically, which was pretty normal for Daniel; sarcasm dripped through him like water through ground coffee beans—slow and purposeful. "What time of day was it?"

"Dude, it was like seven in the morning. I didn't think that I would have to worry about a cop on 123 that early in the day. Especially on a *Sunday!*"

"You always have to worry about a cop on 123," said Daniel. "It's like taxes and death. You know, certain."

Then, suddenly, Daniel looked at me with a quizzical look on his face—as if he was thinking to himself that something didn't add up.

"Matthew, what were you doing in McLean on 123 at seven in the morning on a Sunday?" he asked quickly, laughing a bit at the scenario.

I just looked at him.

Daniel had just asked me the one question that I did not want to answer. I didn't feel like I could answer it—not without admitting that I had slept over at my girlfriend's house the night before. I was certain that would be a fact that would no doubt be extremely disappointing to Daniel, the friend who supposedly kept me accountable.

My girlfriend and I hadn't had sex, though we had certainly done more than simply kiss. And as soon as Daniel found out where I had been, he was going to feel obligated to ask me a lot of questions—questions that frankly I would not feel like answering.

My mind raced to find a quick remedy to my situation. *What am I going to say? What lie am I going to tell to my good friend Daniel?* As I sat scanning my brain for a good story, it felt as if God had emptied my mind of any reasonable lie that might have been convincing to my friend. Still trying my best to stay calm, I could think of no good reason for being in McLean on 123 at seven in the morning on a Sunday—*except for the truth.*

Meanwhile, Daniel was looking back at me with an incredulous grin on his face. "Did I ask a bad question?" he said, taking a sip of his drink.

"Umm … I, uh …" The syllables were stumbling out of me like I was scared out of my mind. The truth about myself didn't scare me. Telling another Christian the truth about me—that's what terrified me.

I didn't mind telling Jesus my problems; he was patient and friendly and known for his forgiveness. But every time I told another Christian, there was always some kind of formula or process or preconceived judgment that you were expected to experience before "forgiveness" would be made official. And most times, there was a waiting period on that forgiveness—I'd have to get approved, sign a contract, and then wait ten days for it to be made legit. I didn't like the process.

But at that moment, I was sick and tired of fearing the official business. And besides, the weight of what I carried *was* consuming my thoughts. So, I took a deep breath, and I just said it out loud with confidence.

"I was over at Laura's house. I stayed there last night."

Daniel just looked at me.

I felt the need to explain just a bit more.

"We didn't have sex," I said. "We've *never* done that. We don't want to do that … I mean, *we do*, but we're not. That, I can promise you. But we certainly did some stuff …"

"I was on my way from her house when I got the ticket. I was speeding because I was late for Sunday school."

Daniel was silent.

His forty-seven seconds of nonreply was too much for me to bear, so I broke the silence.

"Are you going to say something?" I asked seriously. "Do you hate me? I am *so* sorry, bro … I know I should have told you …"

Another minute went by, but to me it felt like twenty. Finally, Daniel piped up.

"Hate you? Do you *really* think I would hate you over something like this?" asked Daniel.

I shook my head no. But actually, I wasn't too sure of the answer to that question.

"You don't *ever* have to apologize to me. As long as I know that you and Jesus are talking through this stuff, I am fine. And by the look on your face, Jesus seems to be speaking rather clearly right now … Listen, bro, I am your friend; I'm here to be a light when you can't 'find your way home,'" said Daniel, using both of his hands to motion air quotes. "Heck, I would expect the same from you."

As Daniel spoke, my eyes began to well up with tears. I'm not sure if it was his response or the heaviness that had just been lifted from my heart, but something moved me. I had rarely experienced "light" like this before. Everything in my spiritual history made me believe that judgment was an extensive and critical part of light, especially the kind of light that shone inside the church walls. At first, Daniel's reaction to my sin confession felt very awkward and strange—like a foreign object that I didn't understand. A part of me believed that I needed to feel the judgment before I could experience the forgiveness of Christ.

After we ate, the two of us prayed. As I drove away, I said out loud in the car, "Jesus, help me remember this; I need to remember this experience. Light doesn't require judgment, and it should be revealed with mercy."

Daniel and I spent many times praying together over the next few months. His time and care and words were much-needed light for me, a desperate traveler.

When the light of Jesus shines through humanity, you never know what it will reveal.

Pause and Reflect

How do you define the "light" Jesus talks about in Matthew 5?

When you think about your own "light of Christ," is it more like a candle or a spotlight?

CHRISTIANS NEED LIGHT

I've heard a lot of chatter about light over the years. Some of it has interested me. Some of it has not. Theologians and preachers, thinkers and poets, writers and musicians have long spent their energy and talent playing in the sandbox with the concept of light. They ask questions: *What is it? How do we show it? Is this way more effective than that? What did Jesus mean when he called us to be light in a dark world?*

I don't have any new theories on light. I don't really have any regurgitated old theories either. All I have is what I have experienced. Just like you, I look to Scripture, prayer, and the words of all those thinkers who are much wiser than me to help me understand how I can be a more effective light for Jesus. When we are on a journey with Jesus, he teaches about light.

Like salt, light can be good and bad. You can reveal too much. You can shine too little. Sometimes we're called to be a spotlight. Other times, Jesus simply needs the gentle glow of candlelight. Those of us who have grown up in Christianity have been inundated with thousands of ideas and illustrations about light.

The geography of where we're supposed to be light often gets debated. I hear the majority of modern Christians talk about the importance of *being* a light in the world. They believe that Jesus' goal for us is to take the message to those who do not know him. "We are the light in the dark places; we need to be sharing the salvation message wherever we can," I heard one man say recently.

And I wholeheartedly agree with all of the people who make this their intent, because I too think it's obvious that Jesus is referring to evangelism in Matthew 5 when he said that he wanted us to be like a city on a hill. But I don't think evangelism is all that he's talking about; I think our light is supposed to shine for anyone who is in need of knowing simple truth, feeling grace, or experiencing generous mercy. I think Jesus intended our light to shine for *all* to see.

I've heard many people unintentionally demean those who feel called to shine light in the church. "You're preaching to the choir," the critics will often say. I'm guilty of using that phrase too. And quite frankly, sometimes it's appropriate. Some people do spend too much of their time inside the safety of the church. But I don't think it helps the cause of Jesus to spend time criticizing such people.

A few years ago, I had a motto for being light: Pursue shining it out into the world. I went out of my way to pursue relationships only with people who had no concept of Jesus. When I was around these individuals, I tried to shine Jesus as best as I could. I was careful not to assume that every person was the same. I invested a great deal of thought into knowing where they were and how I could be most effective at being a light in their lives. But I ended up getting drained—mentally, spiritually, and emotionally. Oftentimes when you're concentrating on *being* light, you forget that you have to take the time to look for light, too. It dawned on me one day that *I* needed light. I needed to see the city on a hill just as much as those who didn't know Jesus needed to see that same city. I needed the light of other believers to shine on me so that I could continue to shine. All of us need to see and experience some good light.

When I experience light, I am experiencing the story of Christ lived out through the lives of each other. I don't know about you, but it thrills me to see Jesus come alive through friends, family, and strangers.

Last year, one of my closest and dearest friends, Lee Steffen, left Nashville to travel the world helping people. I was sad to see him leave the area; many times he had been the local friend who was my sounding board, prayer partner, and fellow dreamer.

But since he's set out on his journey, I have looked for and anticipated his light. Through phone calls, e-mails, and his personal blog, I have gotten to see the God-colors of this world in a way that I would have never witnessed had he not taken this huge leap of faith and followed his heart. Lee's light, all the things that his life communicates about Jesus, fills me up so I can continue to dream, live, and shine Jesus in this world.

Jesus called me to be light. He said for me not to hide it. He said for me to be like a city on a hill. I don't want to be afraid to be that city for both those who believe and those who resist the truth. My friend Daniel reminded me of this by letting Jesus shine through his words that night at Outback. Despite stumbling upon a dark place in my life, he didn't avoid letting me have a glimpse of the light he knew to be true. And I desperately needed to see it.

The church is too often filled with dark places in need of light to appear. Light happens when we proactively look for opportunities to reveal Jesus in the situations where we live. All we need to do is look to see where God can use us to reach people in need of light. If we let ourselves be used, light works.

Light Is Merciful

Ocean City, Maryland, is usually a place people go when they are in search of the warm summer sunshine and mostly naked bodies. But on this particular trip, I wasn't there for the sunshine and ocean water; it was November, and one of the largest seventh- and eighth-grade youth retreats in the country was in town. I had made the trip over from northern Virginia to be a youth leader. Up until that day, I had never really interacted much with seventh and eighth graders. However, all of that was about to change, as I had been chosen to be the "adult" in one of the hotel rooms, where I would be sharing a space with five seventh-grade boys. I had no idea what I was about to encounter.

The experience was less than thrilling for me.

"Did you know that you are going bald?" asked one of the kids bluntly.

"I am? *I had no idea,*" I said, somewhat sarcastically. However, my words were much nicer than my thoughts. I had just recently come to terms with the fact that my hairline was making a beeline for my backside. Denial was still a little bit of a problem for me at that time. I hated that I was going bald. There was nothing cool about it. I was already thinking way too much about it on the inside. Needless to say, I wasn't ready to discuss my hair's desolate future in an open forum—especially with a bunch of harsh seventh graders.

"Do you use Rogaine?" the kid continued.

"That's none of your business," I said.

The kid started laughing out loud.

"That means you do," he joked.

He then pointed to his friend who was jumping ferociously on one of the beds and said, "Hey, Dan, this guy uses Rogaine."

"He needs to, Kevin," said Dan. "If he doesn't, he'll have trouble with the ladies. All bald men have trouble with the ladies."

I thought about retaliating, but I didn't think there was a point. Again, they were seventh graders. So, instead, I self-consciously and covertly checked my hairline out in the mirror, hoping I would feel better. It didn't help.

Then, out of the blue, the conversation among the kids changed.

"How many people think our math teacher, Mr. Dyson, is gay?" asked Dan, yelling so he could be heard over the commotion of the room.

"Dan, we don't need to be discussing that here," I said in a fatherly tone. I hate hearing myself speak in that tone.

"He's *totally* gay," said Kevin.

The others piped up and agreed.

"Well, that's for him to worry about and not us," I said, trying desperately to think up a new subject.

"Hey, guys!" yelled Kevin. *"Let's look and see if our TV gets porn.* Maybe we have *Skinamax!"*

"Sit down, Kevin; you're not looking to see if the TV gets porn," I snapped. Kevin didn't turn on the TV, but he continued to test my patience.

"Hey, Matthew, have you ever had oral sex?" Kevin asked, running back over to jump on the bed.

"What?!" I replied.

"You know, *oral sex!"* Kevin said, indifferently. The thirteen-year-old kid then went on to name off about six other names for it—two of which I had never heard before. He acted as if I had never heard of it before.

"Kevin, I know what it is; I just don't think that this is the place to be talking about that. OK?" I was firm but tried not to be a complete geek, although I felt like I was thoroughly failing.

"Well, I can't wait to get my first …" said Kevin, and then he proceeded to simulate the motion of receiving oral sex.

"Kevin, what are you doing?" I screamed, pushing him off the bed. *"We are at a Christian retreat; we don't act like that."*

I am not made for this, God.

Though I may have come a long way from the stifled bubble of my conservative Christian school education, I still had little clue about the culture of public school kids. These five kids said *many* things that my publisher will not let me write on these pages. At the time, I was not used to this behavior. The youth groups I had helped with before were filled with kids who had been churched and overchurched since they were in diapers. With those kids, ministry seemed easy; they still had the church's idea of innocence and truth very much intact. I had *never* been shocked by what came out of their mouths. But the five boys I stayed with at that retreat were much more informed about the world than I would have ever imagined. Sadly, in certain instances, they were much more informed than I.

After we returned from the weekend retreat, the youth pastor asked me if I would lead a seventh- and eighth-grade small group. I was more than a little hesitant at first. I didn't think I was made for the seventh-and-eighth-grade kind of light. But the youth pastor kept asking me and encouraging me to take a leap of faith and participate.

Finally, I agreed. But I wasn't excited about it.

For three years, every Sunday morning at 11:00 a.m., I gathered with a group of eight rambunctious teenagers and talked to them about God, life, girls, and sex. At first, I was forceful and rigid. I lost two of the kids because of that. That's when the youth pastor told me that I needed to be flexible and not try to force stuff down the throats of these kids. He told me if I would simply back away and let God's light shine through me, good results would come.

So, I pursued being an adaptable sort of light—whatever that really means.

During that study, sometimes all we did was go to Starbucks and chat. That was hard at first. Other times, we opened our Bibles and searched God's Word for clues about what life is truly about. Eventually, I got used to them making fun of me going bald. When they jokingly brought up oral sex or masturbation, I let them talk about it, and then I tried to figure out a way to bring God into the conversation. Sometimes it was successful; sometimes it was disastrous. Sometimes it was light filled.

When I left the northern Virginia area, those guys were in ninth and tenth grade. The night before I left, they took a picture of all of us. One of the kids' mothers had it framed and sent it to me in Nashville. I still have that picture. Over the years, I have often looked at the picture and whispered a prayer for each of those boys. I hoped that someone was being light in their lives.

Last year I had the pleasure of being the speaker for that church's youth retreat. Most of the guys who had been in my small group were in college by then. When I walked into the youth pastor's office, a mother who was going to be volunteering on the trip followed me in.

"Hi, I'm Mary," she said.

"Mary, this is Matthew Turner," said the youth pastor. "He's speaking this weekend."

"You're *the* Matthew Turner?" said Mary loudly. "I have heard *all about* you."

"Really? You have?"

"Oh, gosh, yeah. I am pretty much Kevin's second mom," she said. "He was in your small group. Do you remember Kevin?"

"Of course, I remember."

"You influenced him more than you will ever know. I want you to know that. In fact, he'll be at the retreat this weekend. He's coming up from his West Virginia University to volunteer."

Her words made my heart sing a bit. I didn't say anything out loud, but inside I was dancing a little. It felt good—maybe even *magical.*

When I arrived at the retreat, it was awesome to see Kevin again. He was pursuing his love of Jesus with fervor and hadn't lost any of the vibe that made him so unique. Another guy from my small group, John, contacted me via instant messenger recently just to say hello. He, too, is chasing his dreams in light of the story that God has written on his heart. Dan, on the other hand, hasn't been back to church since he was in tenth grade. The last time I heard from him, he was investing his life into "other things more important to him." But Kevin, John, and Dan are not the reason why I share this story. You learn on the journey that light isn't something that can be measured in successes and failures.

This story is about how sometimes our light has to take on different forms to be effective. Being light is less about the message and more about the person who is watching you. For some people, light comes in the form of honesty. For others, they see it in simple acts of kindness. And for others, they just need a hug.

For the young men in my small group, they wanted to know if a twentysomething guy who was losing his hair could relate to their story. And before I could relate to the stories of these young men, I had to step away from my preconceived ideas about good behavior. I had to alter my preplanned schemes about what spiritual investment looked like. I had to understand that being light means I won't always be comfortable.

Ultimately, I chose to venture out and let Jesus use me in a situation that didn't come naturally to me. My decision didn't instantly make me relate or feel comfortable. Change took time. I learned to adjust the light according to the situation at hand. Did I see a lot of magic happen during those few years? Not really. And for a long time, I thought I was wasting my time. But today, when I'm busy writing on my computer and one of my old small-group guys sends me an instant message to say hello, to let me know what God is doing in his life—that's when I experience the magic. You give light; you get light back.

However, they do still make fun of me for losing my hair.

Pause and Reflect

"Being light" isn't easy. It forces us out of our comfort zones. Reflect on how your "personal light" could be more flexible.

What do you believe Jesus meant when he asked us to be like a city on a hill?

Nobody Said It Would Be Easy

As soon as I picked up my cell phone, I knew by the sound of Daniel's voice he wasn't calling me with good news. I had been waiting for him at a restaurant. He was running late—with good reason.

"Matthew, I can't come to dinner; Jennifer committed suicide this afternoon," said Daniel, obviously fighting back tears. "She hung herself."

"*What?!* Are you kidding me?"

Of course, I knew he wasn't kidding. Decent people don't kid about stuff like that. Unfortunately, I didn't know Jennifer all that well; all I knew was that she was a fourteen-year-old girl who occasionally attended my church's youth group. As I listened to Daniel describe the little detail that he knew, my mind raced back to three weeks before, when I had lost a cousin and two friends in an unforgettable series of events on a Memorial Day weekend. Every death had been separate, tragic, and unexpected. My cousin had died of an aneurysm, my friend in a car accident, and a kid I knew from work had taken his own life. The experience of losing that many people all at once made my own life seem somewhat overrated.

To say the least, that Memorial Day weekend had left me with a lot of questions.

As the news of Jennifer's death traveled, my cell phone began to ring incessantly. But I chose not to pick up the calls. I didn't feel like chatting anymore. So, instead, I began to nervously pace the restaurant parking lot, talking audibly to God.

"Is this your idea of taking care of things?" I asked, as kindly and respectfully as I could. Questioning God was a new concept for me; I had recently stumbled upon new grace that allowed me to ask questions—freely. "You just decided to take someone else? Please tell me, where I am supposed to see faithfulness and mercy in this? Please? I don't see you answering anybody's prayer."

I knew that God had the power to intervene and save someone's life if he wanted to. And the fact that he didn't frustrated me. When my cousin collapsed in front of a toilet and was rushed to the hospital, we had thousands of people praying that God would bring him through his sickness. But the miraculous never happened. And then, when I had heard that the kid I worked with went missing at a Christian retreat he was on, thousands of people had prayed for his safe return. The next day, his body was discovered on the ground near a broken limb and some rope. God had seemingly been absent from the situation. Or at least, that's what I thought at the time.

While I was pacing and talking, my cell phone rang again; this time, it was my friend Lisa, who was also a fellow volunteer in the youth ministry.

"Lisa, I am so sorry," I said as soon as I answered the call. To me, a regular "hello" just didn't seem appropriate.

Lisa said nothing at first; the only thing I could hear was the sound of her sniffling nose in my ear.

"I wish I had the words to say to help make you feel better, but I don't," I said quietly.

There were no good words to say, really. Nobody has anything good to say in this kind of a situation. That balance between saying something and saying nothing at all is a very tangled web. In a moment like that, everything you say seems shallow and stupid, but when you say nothing, it seems careless and unresponsive. Sometimes to a fault, I almost always choose speaking.

"I have a question," said Lisa. "Where do you think God is?"

"I don't know!" I replied in frustration. "Where *is* God in this situation? I've just spent the last fifteen minutes asking him that same question. Where was he three weeks ago when my cousin died? Where was he today when Jennifer tied a noose in her room?"

Lisa interrupted me.

"Mateo," said Lisa, "I think we're asking different questions."

Lisa was getting ready to jet off on one of her intellectual spiritual tangents; I was sure of it. Her intelligence is far above the average church attendee. It's not as though she flaunts it, like others I knew; she simply *is* intelligent, and therefore her faith benefits. And I have to admit, Lisa usually makes a good point.

"*Your* questions imply that God is not here," said Lisa. "*I* was just asking where you thought he might show up? Where he exists. I am sure that he exists in this tragedy. Wherever he is, I want to make him more known, that's all."

"Oh. I don't have the faintest idea, Lisa," I said. "Honestly, I don't really understand any of this. It seems completely absent-minded of God to allow this to happen again in my life."

"Again, I think you might be missing the point, Matthew," said Lisa carefully. "This situation *isn't* really about you. The deaths that happened several weeks ago, although tragic and close to you, weren't about you, either. I just happen to believe that God shows up, and it's our job to reveal him to the best of our ability. That's what being light is about ..."

Lisa's words silenced me. With the phone against my ear, leaning up against a stranger's van, I simply listened.

"... do you know how many people are going to need to see Jesus in the events of the next three days? Hundreds. Are we going to stand here and ask a bunch of questions we may never know the answer to, or are we going to go do what we're called to do? I think we need to be light, Matthew. We need to encourage, pray, and support. A lot of kids are going to need our help to get through this."

Sadly, I have a selfish habit of always trying to find the shortest distance between tragedy and how it relates to me. Actually, I do that with most things.

Lisa was right. This tragedy wasn't about me. God didn't owe me any explanation. He didn't have to answer all of my questions about why he didn't intervene. If I truly loved him, if I truly desired to be used, then I would simply concentrate my life and actions and energy on what he expected of me. That didn't mean it would be easy; it was simply the story he chose to write in my life. I needed to comply. One of the greatest reminders from Jesus on the journey was this: This life isn't about me. It isn't about my story. That was extremely hard for me to learn.

Lisa reminded me that light was the one thing we could offer without having all of the pieces to the puzzles. We didn't have to understand the whys and hows of this event to be light. She said that we needed to focus on being simple candles of peace, prayer, and hope to all the people who would be asking questions and facing sadness during this time. So, that's what we tried to do; Lisa and I focused on being light.

But knowing where to shine light proved a little difficult. Eventually, our light was most effective in Daniel's life. The next few days proved overwhelming for our friend. He felt the weight of being a comforter and companion and pastor to hundreds of people dealing with a needless tragedy. But through this situation, Lisa and I kept focusing on Daniel to keep his heart and mind on truth. We prayed for Daniel. We laid hands on Daniel. Sure, I didn't understand why the power of Jesus hadn't been revealed for Jennifer. But I chose to believe in that power for Daniel despite my feelings and questions. We prayed that power over Daniel's life. In the end, Jesus used him miraculously over the course of those few days. Jesus was in the situation, and Daniel simply helped make him known. And Lisa and I helped make him known to Daniel. He needed to see the city on the hill. We tried our best, through grace, to be like a city.

Those tragedies happened several years ago. Today, I still find the idea of being light complicated and difficult. At times, it's downright impossible for me to even think about revealing Jesus in a situation. But I want to. I want to learn how to make that something I pursue every day. Why? Because I believe in it. I believe in what light does in the lives of other people. It's my desire to be one flickering light in a huge city. When my light is dim, it's my prayer that Jesus makes yours all the brighter, because I hope that when I see your light I will be encouraged to shine again when my life gets hard. And when you see my little candle shining brightly among thousands of others, I hope it encourages you to continue shining, to continue being a part of the city, the city that is giving faraway travelers the welcoming sight of home.

Lisa shone light on me. Together, we shined light on Daniel. And Daniel was given the chance to shine light on thousands—some who believed and some who did not.

It's still often befuddling to me how the soft glow of a candle can be magical. But when I think about what it looks like to travelers, when they see thousands and thousands of candles softly glowing against a hillside—that sight brings hope to them for rest, food, and water. For some, it might even bring about thoughts of home and safety. When I think *those* thoughts, I am reminded about how magical the light of Jesus shining through people can be.

6 humble pie

Humility is like underwear, essential, but indecent if it shows.

—Helen Nielsen

Blessed are the meek, for they will inherit the earth. (Matt. 5:5 NIV)

—Jesus

HUMILIATION

My father has always liked things three ways: fast, close, and cheap. He's never been much for waiting in a line unless he's at Bass Pro Shops. He can't stand driving more than seven miles to any place unless he's going hunting. And he refuses to ever pay full price unless he's buying a new shotgun. As a kid, I was mostly OK with my dad's stiff way of doing things. But once in a while, his self-made creed would seep far enough into my little world that it would interfere with my noblest attempts to be cool.

Just like my father had a creed, when I was a teenager I had a three-point belief statement about life too. I believed I wanted to be cool. I believed I wanted others to think I was cool. I believed if I wasn't deemed cool by others that my life would be ruined.

And the odds were stacked against me, too. I was quite possibly the *uncoolest* individual at my high school, other than the boy with the constant body odor problem and the girl who would fall asleep in class and then talk out loud about the guys she was crushing on. "Cool" was very hard for me to come by.

My voice was high, my frame was frail, and I was about as coordinated as … well, take my word for it, I was *really* uncoordinated. Needless to say, the girls didn't like guys with higher voices and smaller waists than they had. And my dark brown, thick-rimmed eyeglasses didn't help my case for coolness and sex appeal, either.

I hardly remember being able to see without glasses. All three of my sisters had twenty-twenty eyesight. But not me! By the time I turned seven, I had already gone through two pairs of eyeglasses. My personal motto was: If it's in my family *and* it's hereditary, I would end up with it.

As a kid, I was like the drain catcher at the bottom of the kitchen sink. Although I outwardly had a good attitude about almost everything, I was thoroughly convinced God had a cruel way of showing how much he loved me.

When I was fourteen, I was long past due on getting a new pair of glasses. I was still wearing the gold metal-framed ones I had gotten when I was ten. One of my teachers had noticed me squinting and told me to tell my parents to get my eyes checked. Much to my dismay, Dad offered to take me to the doctor.

"Dad, has Mom set up an appointed with my eye doctor?" I asked.

"No, son; *I did.* I called and made you an appointment at the eye doctor in Still Pond. He's right down the street from us."

"Why can't I go to my regular doctor?"

"Eye doctors are all the same; it don't make any difference what one you go to."

"OK, if you say so. When am I going?"

"A week from this coming Wednesday."

"We couldn't get anything sooner?"

"The eye doctor only visits Still Pond on Wednesdays."

"What kind of doctor visits only on Wednesdays? Is he the one from *Little House on the Prairie*?" I asked sarcastically.

"It'll be fine, Matt. Joe from my office goes in there to see him."

"Joe doesn't even wear glasses, Dad."

"Then the doctor must be pretty good, huh?" My dad laughed, but I wasn't amused.

My entire high school career hung in the balance. I already had a voice that sounded like I was constantly inhaling helium; I couldn't afford to have ugly glasses too.

When a week from Wednesday finally came, I visited the eye doctor—the one who was close and cheap. He didn't have to be fast; when something was cheap and close, it almost always made the "fast" part of Dad's creed obsolete.

When the doctor finished the checkup, he told us to go over and look at the selection of frames. We did. And there, right in front of Dad and me, was a grand selection of twenty-seven styles of men's frames.

"Dad, all of these are really ugly."

"Just pick a pair."

"Dad, these are hideous. *Really* hideous!"

"*Pick* a pair, and let's get out of here. How about these? Put these on."

"They're so big; they cover my eyebrows."

"These?"

"No!"

I closed my eyes tightly and prayed. *Lord Jesus, please, when I open my eyes, help me to see a pair of frames that are at least somewhat cool.* I tried on all but one of the twenty-seven pairs; I refused to even look at the pair that looked more like goggles than glasses. Per my father's creed, I ended up choosing the cheapest frames this little Still Pond office had to offer. They cost thirty-nine dollars. And they were ugly, brown, large, and *ugly*.

After I had the glasses for a week or two, my dad sat me down and talked to me about *my* way.

"Life doesn't always go your way, son; in fact, it usually doesn't," said my dad with more conviction than I had ever felt in my short fourteen-year life. When Dad spoke, he had an unfettered passion that I admired. I always looked at him when he talked; his presence demanded it. "You'll understand this one day. Not getting your way isn't easy, but it happens to all of us."

By the time I reached college, I should have been a professional at the concept of being humble. I was easily the most picked-on kid in my high school. (Other than, of course, the boy who had constant body odor and the girl who talked in her sleep.) My high school experiences had made me highly self-conscious. So, when I got to college, I felt like I had the chance to begin anew. At least, that's what I had wanted.

But college brought new trials. Not only did I battle a great amount of spiritual doubt during that time in my life, but I also had another battle to contend with. In certain ways, this battle was harder than facing doubt. It was the battle I had proudly managed to elude all of my teenage years, the battle that made me shudder with fear just thinking about it, the battle that *really* made me fight my pride—*acne.*

By the time I reached my nineteenth year on earth, my face looked like a war zone. Across my forehead and over both sides of my face, I had what looked to be a topographical map of the Appalachian Trail.

Very few people understood my pain. It's not like some of them hadn't experienced acne—but they had been *fifteen* when it happened, not getting ready to hit the drinking age.

When I battled acne, everyone gave me the absolute worst advice on how to get rid of it. I never asked for the advice, but that didn't stop clear-skinned individuals from offering their best words on my complexion dilemma.

"I've heard that taking a blow-dryer and drying your acne every morning after you take a shower helps," said one girl.

"Don't *ever* pop your zits!" said *everybody*.

"Have you ever tried rubbing your face with a pee-filled baby diaper? I hear it really works."

"Before you go to bed, try putting toothpaste on your face."

"Have you ever tried egg whites?"

I tried every one of those home remedies, except one. There was no way I was going to rub a wet baby diaper on my face.

After countless remedies that didn't work, after yelling in front of the mirror more times than I can remember, after all of the clean-faced people's comments about my skin, I finally took drastic measures to handle my acne—makeup. Yes, makeup—*women's makeup*. I figured actors and singers wore makeup on stage to cover up blemishes. Why couldn't I?

So, I went to the drugstore and bought an oil-free bottle of foundation that was as close to my skin color as possible. I had decided that if anyone ever asked me if I was wearing makeup, I would say, "It's a new acne medication that covers up and cleans up my face."

The makeup worked like a charm too. Well, it did until one of my college friends asked me in front of six other guys if I was wearing makeup.

Silence.

An insane feeling washed over me like I was suffering through one of the ten plagues of Egypt. *Wow!* I thought. *I remember this feeling; I had this feeling in high school. This is what humiliation feels like.* It's been a while since I've felt that kind of sting.

"It's medication for my acne," I said with as much confidence as I could muster. Then I quietly and awkwardly walked out of my buddy's room, headed back to my own room, and washed my face.

I walked into my dorm room a different man than I had walked out. Humiliation in front of one's peers changes a man.

When your innermost circle knows your deepest secret, life is never quite the same. Nor should it be.

The makeup incident was never talked about again.

Humble Beginnings

I've had many moments in my life when I wanted to crawl underneath my bed and never come out. There was the time I sang "O Holy Night" on Christmas morning. The entire song was absolutely perfect until I reached the ending high note—the *really* high note—and my voice cracked (well, actually it shattered) in front of the entire church. Everybody laughed. Another time, I was hosting an event in front of a thousand people. When my name was introduced, I proudly walked across the stage, looking out at the large crowd, and then tripped over a guitar cord and fell on my face. Everybody laughed. Humbling moments seem to follow me like my shadow. I guess, in reality, they follow most people.

My family, friends, and I laugh at most of these moments now. They've become stories that are brought up around the Thanksgiving table or get remembered when old friends and I are catching up. They've been retold so many times, I wonder if all of the details are even true. But my memory etches them into my history. They become a part of my identity. They become unforgettable.

I wish that being humbled and embracing humility were the same. But they're not. In fact, they're quite different—almost opposites of each other. Enduring situations that put you in a humbling position is often a bad feeling; it's embarrassing and uncomfortable. But all of those situations that have left me feeling embarrassed pale in comparison to the times God has taught me what it means to live a life of humility.

Few things are more beautiful to me than a person who lives out humility. Meeting a lowly soul who strives with all of her heart at being last in the world is one of the most magical experiences I have had. But a part of me hates these experiences. Through them, God shows me a picture of myself that reveals my pride. Nothing feels more humiliating and dirty than realizing I'm prideful. I hate feeling dirty almost as much as I hate being last.

Pride fuels much of my inability to embrace the teachings of Jesus, to embrace the lifestyle that emits the magic he desires to come out of my life. Most of the hardest lessons in my life come when I fight the inner need to please only me. But with each experience with humility, each time I get a glimpse of the picture that Jesus sees in me, I am faced with the decision of whether to surrender to Jesus or continue depending on my ability. Pride tells me I can remain. Jesus says move. That, in essence, is the conflict of life. Jesus is constantly telling me to get out of his way. My will tells me to stand my ground. While many talk of Jesus' sweet whispers, I've grown accustomed to his loud, forceful tone urging me to stand down.

Pause and Reflect

All of us struggle with pride once in a while. What for you is the most difficult part of pursuing humility?

How would you describe the kind of humility Jesus talks about?

A BAD TASTE OF HUMILITY IN MY MOUTH

A few years ago, Daniel had to confront me. The two of us were doing our normal meal and drinks at Bob Evans, but this one had been planned with a purpose. Daniel was on an uncomfortable mission to talk with me *about me*. So, while I was eating cinnamon pancakes in the afternoon, Daniel cleared his throat.

"I actually need to chat with you about something," he said seriously.

As soon as I heard those words, my heart rate increased 20 percent, my appetite left me, and Jesus told me to shut up and listen. I love when the attention is put on me, but not when it's bad attention. Bad attention stresses me out. And instantly, I had become stressed. My hatred of surprises, especially ones involving my potential wrongdoing, kept me from keeping my mouth closed.

"What did I do?" I asked, rolling my eyes at the mere thought that we were having a conversation such as this one.

"Why are you taking a tone with me?" Daniel asked. "I haven't even said anything yet, and you're all ready to retaliate. This is pretty typical of you."

"OK. What did I do, Daniel?" I repeated myself, this time using a forced smile and sweet tone to disguise my raging blood pressure. "I would certainly like to know what it is I did."

"Don't you think I will tell you?"

"OK, I'm calm," I said, lying through my teeth.

"Two of my friends have made comments about you, Matthew," said Daniel gingerly. I listened intently as my then-somewhat-new friend carefully selected each word as it was coming out of his mouth. "They are offended by your conversations about sex. They find much of your talk to be inappropriate and unnecessary; they're tired of hearing the innuendos ..."

As Daniel talked, a fight broke out inside my mind between me "the jerk" and me "the guy who was pursuing Jesus."

This has got to be a joke!

(Just listen to Daniel.)

How on earth could my conversation have offended someone?

(You talk about sex a lot.)

Sure, I'm an open person.

(Rude and inappropriate is more like it.)

What's wrong with talking about sex once in a while?

(Absolutely nothing with the right group of people. But you talk about it every chance you get. People get tired of that.)

Who among Daniel's friends are legalists?

(Does that really matter? Aren't you simply avoiding the problem with a question like that?)

Daniel continued as the war raged inside.

"They even went as far as to say that unless you change, they don't want to hang out with you anymore."

Fine. I don't need friends like that anyway.

(Actually, you do. You only have, like, two friends. These are Daniel's friends, and you owe them an apology.)

I still can't believe that someone complained about me!

(Stop focusing on you. The whole world doesn't revolve around you. At least you have a friend who is willing to chat with you about it.)

Daniel kept talking. I just stared at him.

"And, man, honestly, you need to think about how your conversation is viewed by God," said Daniel. "He's pretty clear about our words showcasing the condition of our hearts. And sometimes, the way you talk *is inappropriate.* It might be normal conversation where you came from, but it's not around my friends and me. And I don't think I'm being overly sensitive. Just talk to God about it, man."

Sure, Dan, bring God into this conversation. That's just great. Perfect!

(Daniel, way to bring God into this conversation … that's perfect. Nice transition!)

Daniel stopped talking. I waited a couple of minutes to respond.

"Wow!" I said, not knowing really how to reply. But not knowing how to respond certainly didn't stop me from trying. "Honestly, Daniel, a part of me wants to lash out and say that your friends are full of crap. I think it's insane that I would make them feel uncomfortable. I realize I'm an open person, but I think it's a bit ridiculous."

Daniel shrugged his shoulders. "Then lash out, Matthew. What's stopping you?"

"But then I think, perhaps they're right. Perhaps I do take my conversations too far. Perhaps, in the course of running away so far from my legalistic past, I'm in a place where I'm taking the grace of Jesus for granted." I sat there for a second, quiet. "But I need to think about all of this."

"And really, that's all I'm asking," Daniel said.

That conversation humbled me, embarrassed me, and put me in my place; but eventually it led me to a place of humility, confession, and happier friends. Long before I could change my behavior, I had to see a picture of myself. I had to take myself off the pedestal. I had to realize that this life story is not about me. God doesn't want me focusing on my story; he wants me to join his. And if I decide to join his story, that means I have to be concerned for the thoughts of others.

Sadly, humility is not a onetime lesson. It's a place that you have to keep going back to again and again. The lessons get easier if you make the trip there yourself. But if you forget to go or you emphatically stop going, life will remind you. It might take years, but humility always comes around again.

Humility won't leave me alone. Thankfully, not every lesson is confrontational; sometimes, it's simply in putting a humble person in my path that Jesus knocks me off my throne and onto the floor.

Sometimes, humiliation is a beautiful thing.

Humbled

Something about Darlene Zschech moved me.

I've had the sincere pleasure of meeting many artists who make Christian music. And usually, I don't *just* get to meet them; I often have a chance to engage them in conversation. In the past, I've taken this for granted. I try not to anymore. I realize now that, like a painter, a musician's job is to look at life and find a way to communicate its true meaning through art. Now, some Christian artists do this well, while others are, to put it nicely, simply good singers.

But once in a while when I meet someone who creates music for a living, the conversation leaves a mark on me. I love when this happens, because I realize that's the point of a true artist: When they do what artists are supposed to do, they inspire the rest of us.

Honestly, I didn't expect to be inspired by Darlene. When a colleague of mine and I sat down for a conversation with the writer of "Shout to the Lord," we were both a little skeptical—my colleague even more than me.

From the moment we sat down around a small table and began talking, Darlene's kindness and overall sense of spiritual maturity permeated the room. Several times during the conversation, I caught myself thinking, *What does this woman have that I don't, and where can I go and get it?*

Of course, a part of me was also thinking, *If I can actually sense the good in her life, can she sense the bad in mine? Does she know that she's sitting down with two cynical Christian music editors? Does she sense the sin in my life? Is this dear woman sickened by me?*

I didn't know it at the time, but my colleague felt it too. *And that was a big deal.* She was much more cynical than I. When she and I walked into the elevator after our interview was complete, she looked at me and asked, "Did you feel that?" I looked at her and nodded my head yes. Simply put, there was something extraordinarily different about Darlene, something magical that inspired me to walk away from that conversation feeling alive—on fire, even.

My conversation with my colleague continued as we got into the car to leave. Both of us were still a bit dumbfounded.

"What was it about her that is different from so many other artists we meet?" I asked. "It was insane."

"Matthew, *humility*," she said. "She was genuinely humble. I felt *dirty* next to her."

"Me too," I responded.

"*I know*, but in all seriousness, I think she just knows Jesus—like *knows* on a different level than me. You could tell she had spent time with him—*more time than I have*."

I think my friend nailed it. Somewhere along Darlene's journey of faith, Jesus had taught her something about humbling herself in God's sight. And I believe she went to that place often—as often as she could.

Something dawned on me that day regarding humility. I realized that humility accentuates our faith in Jesus. Darlene didn't have to tell me that she knew Jesus; she didn't need to overexplain her stories or conjure up some message in hope of inspiring us. Because of her humility, her *life* inspired us. The message of Jesus was written all over her face.

So often, people who claim to be Christian—myself included—do so much to try to prove they indeed have the light of Jesus shining in them.

We Christians like to advertise that we're Christian. There have been times in my life when I have *loved* telling people I was a Christian. But more often than not, when we go out of our way to impress someone with our spiritual knowledge or our good deeds or our bright lights, our faith is dimmed because of our pride.

That makes a lot of sense. When less of me actually exists in the picture, when I'm not so quick to promote my story, Jesus gets a chance to break through my life, and he tells my story for me. Or better yet, he gets a chance to use me to tell his. The question usually comes down to this: Am I humble enough to let him do either?

I guess it depends on whether or not I am looking for magic. Humility takes my will, my needs, my goals out of the story—that's hard. Sometimes Jesus comes and makes that change for you—that's very hard.

Pause and Reflect

Most would agree that humility is about the condition of our heart. How do you personally get your heart in a place where your mind and actions are humble?

Who in your life would you describe as humble? What attributes does that person have to make you think that?

THE CHANGING FACE OF HUMILITY

Shortly after losing my job as the editor of *CCM*, I had a long conversation about humility with Lisa, who tends to be blatantly honest. She and I met up at Starbucks in northern Virginia. (I was back in the area on vacation.)

"He's got you pegged, Mateo," said Lisa, laughing. I had just told her a story about my recent visit with a friend who is also a therapist. He had jokingly diagnosed me as a self-centered jerk.

"Seriously, Mateo," said Lisa, "that is hilarious! And actually, he might not be too far off."

"What are you saying?"

"I'm saying I think he has a point. You sometimes are self-centered. And sometimes, you're a jerk."

Lisa is one of only a handful of people who can get away with calling me self-centered. Everybody calls me a jerk at least once and means it.

"You're lucky you are leaving for Romania soon," I said. "That's all I got to say. If you weren't going to serve Jesus in a foreign land, we'd be officially not talking right now." I smiled.

"Man, it's good to see you again, Mateo," said Lisa, laughing.

"You too."

This was a normal conversation between Lisa and me. It was quite common for us to sit around for a couple of hours and talk about everything from the weather to movies to our significant others. By the time we finished gabbing, our hot drinks were cold, and our butts were numb from sitting too long. Most of our talks revolved around wrestling with the things of God. This was how we learned more. This was how we sharpened each other. We didn't think we had all of the answers. But that didn't stop us from leaning on each other's knowledge for support. For us, this was the meaning of community.

"What's God been teaching you lately?" asked Lisa, stirring her tea and breathing in its steam.

"Well, it's kind of ironic that I got my official 'diagnosis,'" I said, laughing. "Because lately, Jesus has been teaching me humility."

"Really? Since you lost your big *CCM* job?"

"Yeah, it's been really hard, Lisa. When you lose a job that you pretty much built your world around, it tends to hit you where it hurts. But I've learned a ton through this—humility is tied to so much of my life that this was probably exactly what I needed to learn. With me getting married next year, I'm sure it will be helpful to have really learned a good lesson in humility."

"I'm sure you will learn a lot of lessons in humility—for the rest of your life."

"Yeah, I hope so; I think I'm finally learning how much I need humility in my life. It's so easy for me to think all of this is about me."

"Are you doing better now?"

"I'm better. Once I realized that my world wasn't over, that Jesus truly needed to teach me a lesson, I've been OK. Other people have it a whole lot worse. Sure, I experienced a pretty hard three months. I hit a couple low points where I did and said things I wish I could take back. But I can't. So, I have to move forward with the lessons that Jesus has taught me through this."

"How do you think humility is different to you now?"

"What do you mean?"

"Matthew, this is the first time since I've known you where you haven't had it all together. You actually seem broken. You often work hard at keeping life together. I know from experience that the lessons you're learning now are much different than before. Humility is real now."

"Oh, it's like night and day. I'm only used to temporary humility. And this doesn't seem to be temporary. This is for however long God wants me to be here. And for the first time, I'm OK with that … I know I want to learn how to stay here."

"Where?"

"Umm, well, I guess down in the fetal position … I want Jesus to hear me say that I can't do it on my own. I want to scream it from the mountaintops. I want to put a tattoo on my chest. I *can't do* any of this without his involvement. And if I'm not in a humble and uncomfortable position—*like the fetal position*—I will *always* try to do it on my own and not include Jesus in the process …"

"Fetal position, huh?"

"I'm not even sure that makes much sense. *Does it*?"

"I get it. Although, I'm not sure I'd tell a whole bunch of people you don't know that you're living life in the fetal position."

"It will be just between you and me *and my mother*—'cuz I've already told her."

At Night When I Am All Alone

Sometimes I wake up in the middle of the night with a very full mind.

For some reason, our upstairs neighbor is usually still awake at three in the morning. Don't ask me why. I think she must sleep during the day. I usually hear the fifty-five-year-old's footsteps and then the paw steps of her dog chasing after her down the hallway. My wife and I sometimes lie in our bed and try to guess what our neighbor is doing upstairs. My wife comes up with some hilarious scenarios.

But one thing is for sure: We hope she can't hear us as well as we can hear her.

When I'm awake at night, the railroad that is adjacent to our community will predictably have one train that runs by, tooting its horn exactly three and a half times for all to hear. The train sounds so impressive in the middle of the night—it sounds loud and big and fast. But really, it's just loud. At first, when I moved into this condo, the train bothered me, but now it's a sound that I associate with home. I'd miss it if it were gone.

When I can't sleep, I do what most Christians probably do—*I pray*. My prayers are a little needy at night. But Jesus understands. He likes it when I'm needy—not codependent, just needy. Once in a while, Jesus talks to me at night. I find it so much simpler to hear him when it's dark and I'm alone. We have a conversation. It's in those moments that I tell him to keep me close by his side. I tell him that I am nothing without him. But, of course, he knows all of that.

One night when my wife was away visiting her parents in Wisconsin, I was awake. It's crazy how quickly after marriage it becomes hard to sleep when your wife isn't in bed with you. So, I lay awake, staring at our white textured ceiling. I just began talking to Jesus. We had a conversation, and, yes, I talked out loud.

"What do you want from me, Jesus?" I asked. "What do you really want from me?"

I want you to be a man who is not consumed with fame, wealth, or security. I can use a man like that.

Those were his words back to me. They stung my heart. It's not like I didn't know that; it was just hard to hear it again and then compare it to my life.

"You know how hard that is for me," I replied. "*You know* that kind of life goes against my personality."

You won't ever be that man unless you begin to take on the qualities of my personality, Matthew. You use your personality as a crutch, as a reason not to really follow me. You only dance around with me. But you still haven't truly decided to walk with me.

"You're right; I probably don't."

I keep telling you and reminding you of all the things that truly bless me. But you resist them. You hold back because you like your pride. You like thinking about yourself. You're afraid that following me fully would make you unpopular or make you appear to be a conformist. You know I'm not impressed with the world's opinions. But you are. I see it in your heart.

I stopped talking after that and just quietly confessed. Jesus was right; he's always right. I do hold on to this world so tightly. I didn't think that was a problem with humility, though. I didn't see that how I view the world's perception of me is a *me* problem. But Jesus basically pointed out to me that when I am concerned with what everybody else thinks, I'm putting myself on a pedestal. So again, I stepped down. I have to do that a lot.

Jesus is certainly patient with his kids. But sometimes I've mistaken his patience for contentment. He's not content unless I am moving toward him and then with him. Unless I am craving the humility that he desires, he's not all that impressed.

When I'm meek and humble and let go of myself, I begin to see the work of Jesus in my life. That's the moment where being salt and light makes sense. It's in that place where peacemaking becomes natural. Getting humble, putting myself in that "fetal position" before Jesus, makes a heart pure. Humility is not only a good jumping-off point for relearning Jesus, but it's also the core and completion of magic. Humility is the glow that makes all of our good deeds shine.

I've learned that when I am in a place of humility, I can hear the heart of God. Humility is a place I have to visit often. You don't just suddenly "get there." And when I think I do, it only means I need to go there *again*.

It's a journey.

7
love doesn't have to be a cliché

Truly loving another means letting go of all expectations. It means full acceptance, even celebration of another's personhood.

—Karen Casey

You're familiar with the old written law, "Love your friend," and its unwritten companion, "Hate your enemy." I'm challenging that. I'm telling you to love your enemies. Let them bring out the best in you, not the worst. (Matt. 5:43–44)

—Jesus

MOM'S LOVE

When I was six years old, I still loved sitting in my mother's lap. There was something peaceful about leaning back against her chest with my head nestled against her neck as she gently made the old crackly rocking chair move back and forth. I loved hearing the sound of that old rocking chair; even today, when I hear that distinct noise, I think of my mom. When I was six, I was getting too big to sit there very long. But my mom didn't mind; it was peaceful for her, too.

While I sat there in her lap, she'd whisper in my ear, "Do you know how much I love you? Words will never be able to describe how full my heart is for you."

As a kid, I loved hearing my mom whisper. There was something magical about the way her soft voice tickled my eardrum. Not only could I hear her love, but I could feel it, too. I never once questioned my mother's love for me. She taught me the importance of wearing my affection on my sleeve. Her love for her family was always obvious.

Today, I realize that I learned how to love Jesus from my mom. I've watched her learn over the years what it means to fall in love with her Savior. I was always able to sense when Mom was especially close to Jesus; her time with the Lord always ended up turning into more love for her family. Those are mental pictures that I will never forget.

I know now that those moments in my mother's lap, when I was probably too big to be there, are the first memories of mine where I *felt* love for somebody other than myself. There's something pure and free about the kind of love a kid feels for his or her mom and dad. It's the kind of love that's difficult to say out loud—not because you're embarrassed to say it, but because you haven't learned the words that even come close to describing it. The love that doesn't need words is magical; it's the kind of love that Jesus wants me to show to people—*all people.*

When I was growing up, the concept of "Christian" love was bewildering to me. The "love" I witnessed within the four walls of my church was a form of religiosity that today I wouldn't wish on my worst enemies. The kind of love my church showed could have easily been mistaken at times for abuse, punishment, or carelessness. It was the most unpalatable kind of love I have ever encountered.

When you're focusing on enforcing rules instead of embracing Jesus, love is often the first thing to become deformed and tainted. It's hard for love not to get infected when a church is busy managing the actions and morals of people. When the length of my mother's skirt was more important than what was going on inside of her heart, love became sick. When visitors in my youth group would all get ushered into a room and *every one of them* would come out "born again," love smelled. That's what happens to love when a church focuses on rules.

My old church often went to the extreme with an intense kind of legalism few are privy to. But I still see glimpses of that kind of thinking and behavior in churches today. It's not so much rules like hair length and forced salvation experiences as it is the spiritual expectations put on people. Whether it's using speaking in tongues as a barometer for faith or making small-group involvement the end-all-be-all for community or overprogramming the lives of Christians with seminars, conferences, and studies, the church is still notorious for presenting faith in Jesus as a formula or equation for the content life. If we're not careful, the "equation" becomes the focus, and in the process, love begins to smell funny. Sometimes it just plain stinks. I have seen the effects of infected love over and over again in the stories of people who have become victims of church gone wrong.

When I hear such stories, my heart aches at the awful way Jesus is being represented to people. Religion can be so cruel. When people are spiritually abused, it's a very deep kind of pain because it hits what often is the core of people—their faith. When a person's faith is infected with poor teaching, sexual abuse, legalism, and the absence of love, the effects are devastating. I know those effects.

But I don't want to mislead. Despite all that I saw in the church, it's not like I didn't *know* love as a kid; the love that held my family together was a spiritual and relational kind of love. Just as I was able to watch my grandmother be the truth of Jesus in my life, I saw that truth in my parents and sisters. They were *far* from perfect. But my mom and dad's love for my three sisters and me was the one thing I *never* questioned. I'm convinced it's their love that kept me sane through it all. I watched them *try* to bring a little love and mercy into their church life. They strived to love like they believed Christians were supposed to love, but the rigid nature of legalism always crept in and would overwhelm us. Eventually, we, along with other families in the church, stopped trying.

We left.

Pause and Reflect

Why do you think loving people is so difficult for some Christians? How is it difficult for you?

What are your limits regarding love? In other words, how far will your love go?

AFFECTED BY THE EFFECTS

As a young adult, I struggled with being a Jesus follower because I didn't understand his spiritual command for us to show love. In fact, it goes deeper than even that: I didn't understand God's love. I knew that he loved me enough to send his Son to die, but I had a hard time understanding his fatherly love, his love as a friend, his love as someone who would never leave me or forsake me. As far as I was concerned back then, he hadn't kept up his end of the bargain. I thought he *had* left me. I thought he was crazy for conjuring up this ridiculous way of following. I didn't understand the truth back then. Now that I am an adult, I can certainly look back and see where Jesus didn't forsake me or leave me; but as a kid, as a teenager, as a college student, even in the early parts of my new journey, I was blind to that.

By the time I entered college, I knew more about how to hate sin and sinners than I did about how to show the love of Jesus. And when you have experienced an infected type of love for more than seventeen years and invested a great deal of time into hating sin and those who sin, every aspect of your spiritual life is affected. My understanding (or lack of understanding) of the love of Jesus influenced the way I looked at life, tragedy, friends, dating, evangelizing, romance, missions, church, and service. My inability to love crippled my faith.

Realizing and understanding the truth of Jesus certainly helped. Eventually, I most definitely began to experience the love that Jesus extends to his kids. But even after all of those beautiful moments with Jesus, breaking the old habits of hate and refocusing my Christian life toward loving people was a strenuous and overwhelming journey.

Unfortunately, I wasn't able to change this kind of behavior overnight. Before I was able to show anything that closely resembled the love of Jesus, it took years of seeing and experiencing how Jesus used the love of Christians in the lives of people. I had to see *how* that love worked in people's lives. But after I saw its effects, I then had to accept that work as the love of Jesus and convince my brain not to think of it as a fabrication of his love.

Like most of my journey, that was hard. (I wish I had a dollar for every time I said the journey was hard.) It was hard because often I saw the love of Jesus break some of the rules that I once held in high esteem. *Love can't do that!* I thought. *Christians shouldn't be there!*

When I watched his love (through people) go into bars, hold a gay man with AIDS, sit down with a prostitute and ignore the weed sitting on the table, and embrace an atheist as a friend, it scared me. It's not that I didn't think it was beautiful. On the contrary, it was the most beautiful sight I had ever seen. But when I saw it, my old way of thinking, my old way of believing, would creep to the surface and make me doubt that the love of Jesus displayed through people would go *that* far.

The process of embracing a life-filled, Jesus-focused love was often extremely complicated. My heart needed to be cleaned. It had to be stripped of all that ailed it and then filled with something new and fresh and clean.

Like a Chicken Coop

I once heard a preacher describe his heart as like an unkempt chicken coop. I knew exactly what he was talking about. In fact, I probably understood his illustration better than most—I once raised chickens.

People laugh when they hear that I grew up around chickens. "*You* had *chickens?!*" most say, acting as if they've never met a poultry-savvy individual before. My family didn't have a farm; we owned five acres of land in a rural part of Maryland. My dad has always dreamed about having a hundred-acre farm with cows and cornfields and chickens. Perhaps as a way of living bits and pieces of that fantasy, but also to teach me hard work and the value of money, my father bought me twelve chickens. (I eventually had just over a hundred.)

I was seven years old at the time, and I raised the chickens, harvested the eggs, cleaned the eggs, and sold them to the nice elderly women at church. I had most of my chickens named and knew their faces by heart. And they helped me get to college—in the four years that I sold eggs, I raised nearly $7,000. Of course, my father had probably invested more than that in just feeding those birds. But he didn't care; I learned a lesson, and he got a minifarm.

Cleaning out the coop was my least favorite part of having chickens (that, and when the rats would come out at night). Removing the manure was a half-day event for my father and me. With pitchforks and shovels, the two of us would go into my poop-filled chicken coop and clean it out.

The first pitchfork full of dung would release an awful scent in the air. It was sometimes so nauseating to my seven-year-old nose that I'd have to run outside for some air and coax myself to go back inside. That odor of aged chicken manure had a hint of ammonia to it, and after being penetrated with a pitchfork, the aroma would fill that small area quickly. Underneath the manure, I'd find bugs and worms and mice and other things that lived in the excrement of chickens. Just thinking about the bugs and stench makes the hair on the back of my neck feel tingly. My dad and I had to run all of the chickens out of their house, because they loved pecking and scratching around their freshly turned manure. Those chickens would eat almost anything if you let them. Many of them would stand right outside the door, pecking on the door as if they knew we were doing something incredible inside.

The next nine shovelloads of chicken poop would release the same stench as the first one. But the longer my dad and I worked, the easier the job became, and the less offensive it smelled. After every bit of manure was cleaned out and piled high in the back of my father's pickup truck, I'd spread fresh, clean straw all around the chicken coop. I learned to love and appreciate the smell of clean straw. When I'd finally let the chickens back inside their clean home, I'd stand back and watch them. I swear they acted excited about the good smell, the new straw, and a clean slate in which to do their business.

That preacher I heard was right. My heart has been like a manure-ridden chicken coop on many occasions. Throughout my life, I have found my heart on many occasions to be overcome with "crap." The crap is everything from bad theology to pornography to selfishness to poorly chosen relationships. Anything that alters the scent of my heart.

By the time my family and I left the church of my youth, my heart had been filled with a lot of junk. Over time, the hate and legalism I experienced turned into bitterness and an unwillingness to forgive. Add a little more time, and my heart eventually became full of cynicism, distrust, and doubt. But the one result I remember the most was an inability to love. Eventually, Jesus came in with his pitchfork; the stench of his first shovelful was toxic. Of course, when he began to overturn my filth, I wanted to poke around. I wanted to collect a few souvenirs. I wanted to see if I could find anything interesting. He'd run me out. He'd remind me that there is nothing here for me.

But before I went through the process of surrendering and allowing Jesus to clean out my heart, a lot of people came in contact with a smelly mess.

Pause and Reflect

Jesus spoke about love coming from the heart. What do you think that *really* means?

In what ways can we as Christians "clean out our hearts"?

WATCHING LOVE

Erin, a girl I met at my first job out of college, knew something I didn't know about loving people. We met all kinds at the restaurant where we worked together. And by that time, I was certainly trying to learn what it meant to love people like Jesus loved them, but I found it often hard and cumbersome. But Erin didn't seem to have too much trouble. Her love for people, no matter where they came from or what they were investing their lives into, seemed to almost seep out of her pores.

Looking back, I believe I learned more about the love of Jesus from Erin than I had learned the twenty years I had been going to church. Investing herself into the lives of hurting and needy people is what Erin did, and once in a while, she'd invite me along for the ride.

"Hey, Matt," said Erin one evening after our shift. "I'm going over to Samuel's house tonight to hang out; want to come?"

I wanted to go, but it wasn't to hang out with Samuel. I wanted to go only because I had a crush on Erin. From the moment I had first laid eyes on Erin, I had been thinking somewhat dirty thoughts about her. I'm not necessarily proud of that fact, but I'm being honest. I decided to go, despite the fact that Samuel and everything he stood for frightened me out of my mind.

On the drive over to Samuel's, Erin and I chatted about why she hung out with this guy so much. As always, Erin was blunt, but as sweet as southern iced tea.

"He's a nice guy," said Erin softly. "Why shouldn't I hang out with him, Matthew?"

"I don't see anything wrong with befriending him at work," I said. "He *is* a nice guy. But I just think he's more apt to rub off on you than you are to rub off on him."

"You're beginning to sound like a Christian, Matt," said Erin, still wearing her pretty grin. "Samuel is gay, Matthew; he's not contagious."

"Well, that's not *exactly* true, Erin," I replied. My comment seemed more appropriate inside my head than when I actually opened up my mouth and said it out loud.

Erin's mouth opened wide in shock.

"Matthew Turner!" she said. Then with about as much sarcasm as Erin could muster up, she quipped, "Well, unless I'm planning on having sex with Samuel, which I do believe he might be morally against at this time in his life, I doubt I'll be catching what he has. You're as stupid as you are hilarious."

I felt much more stupid than I did hilarious. But as stupid and immature as I probably came across to her over and over again, Erin never treated me with any less love. I guess she figured I needed as much love as anyone.

When we arrived at Samuel's house, he answered the door wearing nothing but a pair of yellow and green briefs.

"*Oh my gosh*, guys, come on in," he said. "I just jumped out of the shower. I had no idea what time it was. Let me put on some pants and a shirt."

When he left the room to dress, Erin squeezed my hand and smiled. I just rolled my eyes in embarrassment. "I can't believe he answered the door like that," I whispered into Erin's ear.

"That's Samuel," she said, still grinning.

As Samuel was getting dressed, I looked around his house. It was like a museum. Statues and paintings and small glass figurines covered his living room. I counted three pictures of Jesus on his walls.

"Hey, Samuel," I said, yelling so he could hear me in his bedroom, "why do you have so many pictures of Jesus hanging on the wall?"

"*Jesus is a hot* ______ ______," he said loudly.

When I heard all of those words used in one sentence, my jaw dropped.

Erin gave me a look that said, *Keep your fat mouth shut, Matt*. So, I said nothing, although I was pretty certain that our little gathering would be coming to an end shortly because God had undoubtedly turned Samuel into a pillar of salt for talking about Jesus *and* Mary like that. But alas, the mercy of God was proved once again when Samuel's door swung open.

"Sorry, guys," said Samuel, walking into the living room. "Have a seat and make yourselves comfortable."

Erin ran over to Samuel and gave him a big hug. He hugged her back but picked her up so abruptly that the two almost fell over onto the floor. And after they had finished doing a *waltz* in the middle of the floor, the *happy couple* sat down next to each other on the largest futon I had ever seen. I walked over to the only seat left in the room; after eyeing it over thoroughly, making sure it was clean, I sat down rather uncomfortably.

"Samuel, do you have a candle or incense burning?" I said, smelling the air.

He laughed an obnoxious laugh and then simply said, "No."

"OK. I smelled something sweet in the air; I thought it might be a candle or whatever."

Suddenly, after I had finished talking, there was an uncomfortable silence in the room. I could have cut the tension with the fake sword that Samuel had fittingly placed between the legs of a plastic Abraham Lincoln statue.

With Samuel unable to see her, Erin looked at me with a smile, held her hand close to her face, and gave me what I thought was the "OK" sign. She obviously knew I wasn't getting her signal, so she made the same gesture three times. But still, I had no idea what she was trying to communicate to me.

"Erin's trying to tell you that I smoked pot before you got here," said Samuel, bluntly. "That's what you smell."

Again, I felt like an idiot. By that time, I was wishing I had gone home to bed and not come out with Erin. Crush or no crush, my gut told me that this embarrassment wasn't worth it.

"So, what in the world are two good Christians doing out here on the *east* side of town?" asked Samuel with a laugh.

The voice inside me had been wondering the same thing.

"Oh, Matthew and I just got out of work, and we wanted to come by and say hello."

"Well, that was nice of you guys."

The conversation that followed I *mostly* just observed. But it quite possibly could have been the heaviest conversation I had ever witnessed. Samuel wasn't afraid to open up and share. In fact, I learned things about him that I'm *still* embarrassed to say out loud. *And it takes a lot to embarrass me.*

But eventually, the conversation went from sex and drugs and partying to a deeper topic. Samuel displayed his life like it was a new T-shirt he was wearing. He just blurted his story out for two near strangers to hear. It was almost as if he had been craving a *real* conversation for a very long time.

Samuel told us that only six months before, he had been suicidal; his then lover had rushed him to the emergency room after he had swallowed a few pills. But then he claimed that he had done it all for the sake of drama. "I needed a little excitement in my life," he said.

He told us about a boyfriend he had lost to AIDS just over a year before. Then he jokingly said, "I guess, according to you guys, we'll be able to get together again in hell." But as quickly as the laughs came, the tears began to roll down Samuel's cheeks when he admitted that he was afraid to die.

I sat there, mesmerized by Samuel's words. He kept switching back and forth between dramatic emotional pain and a sick sense of humor. Sitting in my chair, hardly able to move, I just watched Erin.

"Samuel," whispered Erin, "come here. It's going to be OK."

She wrapped her arms around his body. Samuel put his face against her left shoulder and just cried. Erin was whispering something into his ear, but I couldn't tell what she was saying. After ten minutes, Erin let go. Samuel wiped his eyes dry.

"I am sorry about this, guys," said Samuel. "I'm sure you didn't think you would end up spending your evening like this."

"Samuel Potts!" said Erin. "You better not think another thought about all of this. You know I love you."

Erin patted his knee.

"Hey, Samuel," said Erin, with more love than I had witnessed in a long time, "I don't want to make you feel uncomfortable, but I was wondering if you might allow Matt and I to pray with you this evening."

"Please do."

Erin prayed for Samuel that evening. Well, actually, it was morning: 1:12 a.m. We sat there and prayed together for more than thirty minutes.

Over the next five years, Erin and Samuel remained very close. Samuel continued to live his life, and Erin continued to love him. A couple of years ago I got a phone call from Erin. "I just called to tell you that Samuel has fallen in love with Jesus," she said to me.

"He has?"

"Yep."

"He called me last week to tell me that he began following Jesus a month ago. Isn't that amazing?"

It was amazing, and it left me in disbelief; even though it was five years later, and I was a very different person, I still felt a little embarrassed. But of course, though I believed her story about Samuel to be true, I first had to ask her if "falling in love with Jesus" simply meant that he had added another photo of Jesus to his collection.

"Matthew Turner!" she said with a laugh.

"It was just a joke; you know I have to make jokes."

Samuel was simply one of twenty people I witnessed Erin loving. I watched her love a satanist. I watched her love an addict. I watched her love a drag queen. But perhaps I was most impressed that, despite the fact that I was a recovering legalist with a knack for making Jesus comments at the most inappropriate moments, she even loved me. I am convinced that I know Jesus more intimately because of Erin.

This Is What My Love Feels Like

I've learned lessons about love throughout my pursuit of Jesus. I believe most Christians have. Life has taught me that becoming a Christian (which, of course, means Christlike) is, like my faith, not a place that I suddenly arrive at; it's more like an expedition. The more artifacts of truth that I discover along the way, the more like Jesus I desire to become.

My most extravagant awakening to the love of Jesus came during a very difficult time in life—when I battled depression. There was something incredibly funny to me about saying, "I am depressed," out loud. In fact, when I first looked in the mirror and said those words to myself, it felt like I was delivering a punch line to a somewhat-funny joke. But I laughed. I stood there, looking at myself in the mirror, and I actually laughed. Truthfully, I had *felt* depressed before, but I had never said the words out loud. That would have been unpardonable for me before that day.

Maybe I laughed because depression came *after* Jesus had brought me out of legalism. Because if there were ever a time that I should have admitted depression, it would have been years earlier when I was fighting my belief in Jesus. Maybe it was funny because I was considered by many to be spiritually mature and together. That's actually even *funnier* for me to say out loud. Maybe it was because I couldn't *really* pinpoint why I was feeling anxious, codependent, and insecure. Nonetheless, despite the fact that I was content in my relationship with Jesus, I had many of the classic symptoms of depression. And to me, it *was* funny, but the comedy wore off in a day or two.

I've often heard that two things happen when you realize you're depressed. Either you run directly away from what you believe to be true or you run toward it. For some reason, certainly not any doing of my own strength, I got closer to Jesus during depression. I'm not saying that the journey was simple or uncomplicated, because in many ways it was dreadful. But Jesus ran as fast as he could to remind me of what was true. For a year, Jesus and I together climbed the mountain toward sanity. Oh, I definitely tried to lose him a few times, because he liked the steep parts of the mountain, but I had no such luck.

But through the harshness that is depression and through the climb that Jesus forced me to experience, I *finally* reached a summit of sorts, and it was a flat road where Jesus and I could convene without interruption, without rope, without me being completely exhausted. Once I reached the easy road and got a good look around,

I wanted to stay there. I looked at Jesus and begged him to let me set up a tent.

There, on the plateau, I grew spiritually. Some people take advantage of these experiences and coast, and I'm certainly prone to, but that time I didn't. I let Jesus teach me new and wonderful things about himself. For months I just sat in his lap. I leaned back against his chest and rested as he gently moved the "rocking chair" back and forth. He whispered in my ear, *Do you know how much I love you? You can't imagine the love I feel when I look at you.*

As I sat there, feeling so comfortable, so at peace, so *not* anxious, I was jarred out of the experience when I felt the rocking stop. Jesus' body moved in such a way that something inside of me was startled. I felt his hands move. His legs shifted.

I thought to myself: *I know this feeling.*

When I was six years old and I had been resting in my mom's lap, the phone would ring or dinnertime would come, and my mother would lovingly and carefully move me out of her lap.

Surely, Jesus wasn't doing that.

My heart raced. I was tempted to panic. *I must be mistaken; Jesus can't be tired of me just yet.*

But sure enough, Jesus wanted me out of his lap. The motions I felt were purposeful and for my benefit. I must admit, I was stunned for a moment—it didn't make much sense. I figured this must have been how the disciples felt when Jesus told them that he would be leaving them soon. They wanted to know why. They had questions. They feared. A couple of them were angered and befuddled. Peter even charged that he would not let that happen. That's when Jesus looked at him and said, "Get behind me, Satan."

As I felt that experience coming to an end, I got one clear message from Jesus during that time. His words were simple and straightforward: *The healing I give is a part of the journey. Now, take this most recent experience of the fullness of my love and share it—just share it, Matthew—I promise to do the rest.*

While I sat quietly in the middle of my living-room floor, two candles were lit on the TV counter, and Bach was softly playing in the background. My face was flat against the black rug that sits in the center of my room. I lay there overwhelmed by the presence of God, dumbfounded by what he had taught me the last few weeks.

The words that Jesus had said to me were scrolling over and over inside my brain. I meditated on them. Suddenly and only for a moment, this feeling of ache and frustration and passion and affection consumed me. The sensation hurt and felt good all at the same time. And Jesus just said to my heart, *That's only a small taste of what I feel for the people of this world.* For barely a moment, my spirit got a small glimpse of how deeply and intensely Jesus loves people. As the weight lifted off me, I wondered if I could have handled much more.

For several years I had known that I was supposed to love people, but there in that moment, I understood *why*. It's not because it's the right thing to do. It's not about looking good to the world. It's not so I can feel good about myself. It's not about publicity and fame.

It has nothing to do with me.

I am to love people—all people—because Jesus loves people.

The process is so frustrating at times because, like everything that Jesus teaches in Matthew 5, I have wasted so much time trying desperately to make it about me. But ultimately, that's the message he communicates to me again and again—this life I live isn't about me. It's not about my satisfaction, my wealth, my health, my book deal; the message that I learned in Matthew 5 is that life is about being a part of his story through loving people the way Jesus loves.

I think Philippians 2 says it much better than I:

> If you've gotten anything at all out of following Christ, if his love has made any difference in your life, if being in a community of the Spirit means anything to you, if you have a heart, if you *care*—then do me a favor: Agree with each other, love each other, be deep-spirited friends. Don't push your way to the front; don't sweet-talk your way to the top. Put yourself aside, and help others get ahead. Don't be obsessed with getting your own advantage. Forget yourselves long enough to lend a helping hand.
>
> —verses 1–4

An Ending Thought on Love

Love is hard. Even today, Jesus continues to stand inside my often crap-filled heart, and with a pitchfork he cleans up the mess that gets left behind by life. Each time he finishes, he spreads out a new portion of his grace and mercy, so I can begin to love again. And I do—I accept the gift and move on. I can't love others without accepting the gift myself.

Jesus says that it's easy to love those who love you back—even those who do not know him do that. "But I say, 'Love your enemies,'" said Jesus. That request has been the hardest of all lessons on this journey. It's hard for me to swallow; it's even harder for me to put into practice. When I think that someone has treated me poorly, it's hard to offer love back. Most of the people I have considered enemies in the past have been church people—people who are supposed to be striving to love.

When love finally captured my heart, I had to spiritually observe my life as if I were a spectator. I had to mentally reintroduce myself to all of the people whom I felt hatred toward, all of those whom I had long since forgotten about. One by one, as Jesus brought them to my mind, I realized how much he loved them and that I was to love them too. Some of those people I have been able to make amends with personally. With some I have lost contact. And honestly, there are a couple of people I'm still trying to love. If I were to see them, the pain of life would come back. But I'm not satisfied feeling like that, because I crave the freedom that comes to those who love. But that comes with learning that the Christian life is an expedition, not a destination.

Freedom comes when I love enough to let go of the pain that has turned into the inability to forgive, that has turned into bitterness of the heart, that has often become personal skepticism about the church. The more I love, the more freedom I experience, because to show love in this world is all about being humble, hungering for truth, showing mercy, pursuing a pure heart, being light, being salt, and being a peacemaker.

I believe it's those ingredients that make love magical for the people of the world to experience and very difficult for some to resist.

8
a journey

Why is it that every time I'm with you makes me believe in magic?

—author unknown

In a word, what I'm saying is, Grow up. *You're kingdom subjects. Now live like it. Live out your God-created identity. Live generously and graciously toward others, the way God lives toward you. (Matt. 5:48)*

—Jesus

OH YEAH, GRACE

When I sat down on the hard wicker sofa and he sat down in his comfy leather chair, I felt like I was about to get a psychological exam. Maybe I was. It certainly seemed possible that his eyes, as they gazed at me over his thinly rimmed glasses, might be able to see inside my soul. His concentrated stare made me feel a little awkward. It felt as though I was living a dream I often had that involved a naked me speaking in front of a thousand laughing circus clowns. At the beginning of the chat, I was tempted to try to overcompensate for what he might be thinking about me, especially if indeed he was psychoanalyzing me.

The man who I was talking to that day is a pretty well-known preacher. He's a kind man, but that doesn't make this doctor of theology any less intimidating. His church is moderately large, he's known around his city for his profound understanding of grace, and I have respected his wisdom about faith for many years. Oh yeah, and he doesn't want me to use his name in my book. But ironically, our conversation last year ended up being the jumping-off point for this book. I believe that a few of his answers really helped me grasp a fuller understanding of what Matthew 5 is about.

Matthew: What's the first thing that comes to your mind when you hear someone say, "Sermon on the Mount"?

Unknown Preacher Guy: A near-impossible lifestyle. *I'm kidding.* Actually, for me the Beatitudes were no doubt the hardest of topics that I ever taught about in my church. So, the first thing I think about is all of the work that I put into it that series.

Matthew: Anything else?

UPG: And I often think about the Grand Canyon.

Matthew: *Why?*

UPG: Whenever I read the Beatitudes, I feel like there's a massive gap between what Jesus expects of me and who I actually am. I feel I am on one side of the canyon looking at Jesus on the other side, and I am unable to reach the other side without his assistance. That's what I sometimes see in the beginning verses of Matthew 5—on the other side of the canyon there is this life that I am called to live, but it seems so far away. So, I end up feeling very helpless. Which I think is the point of Jesus' message in Matthew 5—we are helpless without Jesus … and I constantly compare myself to Matthew 5. And when I do, I pretty much realize again that I suck at being like Jesus.

Matthew: Do you think Jesus intended for us to compare our lives to Matthew 5?

UPG: Well, I believe when a person rereads Matthew 5, you can't help but run an inventory of your life as you read about Jesus' desires for his followers. But to answer your question: No, I don't think Jesus began his ministry with the greatest sermon ever recorded so we would have more guidelines to follow. Jesus was quite aware that guidelines weren't going to work. I think it's important for us to see that the statements Jesus declared that day on the mountain are not a "new" Ten Commandments … but here's the catch: My flesh loves to compare and contrast. It comes naturally for me to look at these statements and try to live up to their depth. In fact, I do it all of the time. *Why*? Because looking at the Sermon on the Mount as a rule book or as a list of expectations is a lot simpler for Christians to understand and to accomplish than it is for us to lean back and depend fully on the grace of God.

Matthew: But Jesus does care that I live a life of mercy and purity, right?

UPG: Absolutely! But you see, Matthew, we go about it all wrong. Too often we actually try and pursue on our own these "qualities" that Jesus longs to see in us. But we cannot. Jesus is hoping that his kids become so compelled by his grace, so mesmerized by his gift of salvation, that these principles in Matthew 5 over time become a natural part of one's life … following Jesus.

Matthew: But it doesn't come naturally for us, does it? I mean, is a pure heart really normal for human beings?

UPG: You're talking to a Reformed thinker, Matthew. [Laughs.] No, I don't believe that a pure heart is something we can strive for on our own. But as Jesus draws us to himself, and as we get to know him, a pure heart becomes more and more possible because of the grace we are experiencing. It's rather simple, really—the more we tie our lives into Jesus and the things he is passionate about, the more *like*

Jesus we are able to live. It's not about walking into a situation and saying over and over again, "I want to be humble; I have to be humble; I will be humble." You're only a few notches away from legalism when you try to embrace the teachings of Jesus like that. There's not necessarily a secret or equation to living out the magic of the Beatitudes; a person just needs to desire it.

Matthew: What's your best advice on pursuing humility?

UPG: Drink daily from the cup of grace, Matthew. I believe wholeheartedly that grace is the key to living this life that Jesus speaks so passionately about. Jesus knows that we are unable to be humble or peaceful without him. That's why grace is imperative. *But* that doesn't mean Jesus will refrain from kicking us in our butts when we're *not* being merciful or humble. He *often* uses a little "influence" to wake us up to drink from his grace, and as we drink, the easier it becomes to reveal mercy, peace, and humility.

Matthew: So, you're saying that living this life is more about the journey than it is about trying to get it right.

UPG: Matthew, if you spend your life trying to get it right, you'll fail every single time. But just remember this: The fact that you're asking these questions means you're on that journey. That's the kind of heart that Jesus can use. Jesus will open the eyes of those who are engaged in the process of truly wanting to live like him.

Foundations

Let's suppose that Jesus decided to come and give the Sermon on the Mount during the early years of the twenty-first century. Imagine for a moment that you are on the mountain the day when Jesus speaks the words of his famous sermon recorded in Matthew 5—7. You're there with a group of friends. Think of yourself as simply one of thousands, maybe millions, in a crowd hearing this would-be Messiah speak words, thoughts, and opinions you have never heard before. Consider the impact this God-man's authority would have on your heart as his words scrape against all that you believe or have heard before. His words offend you; they offend your politics, your morality, and your religion.

Imagine what your reaction would be when you hear Jesus say out loud for the first time that you are supposed to love your enemies, turn the other cheek when someone punches you in the face, and be a peacemaker when you desire to fight back. Your heart and mind would no doubt be filled up with some kind of emotion, some kind of movement. Perhaps you're quite angered because his words contradict what your pastor or priest said the Sunday morning before. Or maybe you're surprised, shocked, and bewildered that he is so honest and up front about the human condition. You might think he should mind his own business and go back to where he came from. His teaching might have mesmerized you. Or it might have simply moved you to cry. No matter what you're feeling or thinking at the time, you walk away knowing this man, this God, is someone you want to know, someone you want to hear more about. His message intrigues you.

If your response is anything like mine, you're probably getting a small taste of what you felt when you heard the gospel of Jesus Christ for the first time. Remember your curiosity? Remember how it upset you? Remember the excitement that welled up inside you when you first felt the Spirit move you? You could hardly contain yourself, right?

The first time I remember being moved to respond to the message of Jesus, I was a child. I sat in the pew with this eager and electrified nervousness running through my body. The need for repentance and redemption ran heavy through my veins. I didn't understand it, but it was there. I responded. I responded with tears. I responded with excitement. Although I certainly didn't comprehend the power that I was introduced to that day, I do remember leaving that moment changed.

Over the years, my heart for Jesus has swayed a bit. Parts of my journey have been poorly chosen pathways and shortcuts. And there have been moments when I've climbed staircases when I should have been enjoying slides. But through it all, I've felt the power of Jesus as he walked alongside me as my guide on this journey. I've heard him speak. I've felt his disciplining hand against my backside. I've sat in his lap. And I've run from him. In other words, I've lived life.

Through it all, one thing has not changed: My faith is provocative. You may question why I would use the word *provocative* in a book about faith. I use this word because I know that if the life of a Christian reflects anything close to what Jesus intends, the result is provocative, controversial, stimulating, and confrontational. When a follower of Jesus loves his enemy, the world listens. When a follower of Jesus decisively makes a choice to be last, communities watch in awe. When a follower of Jesus works as a peacemaker instead of creating more problems and more walls, the office is suddenly shocked. Why do all these things happen? Because when we respond the way Jesus asks us to, our actions grate against the norm. Suddenly, the kingdom that Jesus spoke so passionately about is happening in front of you. And if that's not power, I don't know what is.

Jesus gave us a guideline in his words for kingdom living. Now, the world scoffs at such wisdom. And even churches often make light of Jesus' more provocative statements. But the fact is that either what Jesus said when he was here on earth is completely true, or we are wasting our time. The apostle Paul said as much in his letter to the Corinthians, when the church was questioning some of its more extravagant and controversial beliefs. If that's the case, Paul said, if the challenging, extreme, and controversial truths of Jesus' words are not truths, then "we are to be pitied more than all men" (1 Cor. 15:19 NIV). If these words are not true, Paul said, then our lives are worthless and pitiful, because these words, these truths, have formed the foundation of our lives and our ministry.

What about you? Where would you be if the truth of Jesus' claims and guidelines were taken away from you? I believe too many of us would still have a foundation to stand on, because we've built our foundations on something else—on the comfort of our family, on knowing the right words to say or the right face to wear, on getting a good job and collecting material things, or on finding good friendships and relationships to enjoy. All of those things can be good, and many of them can form a comfortable base for your life. But none of them will lead you to a powerful and provocative faith. And none of them will lead you into the purpose that God made you for.

Yes, it is frightening, and, yes, it is a risk to truly build your life on the words of Jesus and on a relationship with him. But that is the only foundation that will take you walking on the water and make the waves into a place as safe and secure as solid ground. It is the only foundation that will make you into a person who is provocative, who is always challenging those around you to grow and to become more real. It is the only foundation that will make you into the whole and authentic person you were truly meant to be.

Another Journey

I've been relearning Jesus for many years now. When I began the journey, I didn't realize that "relearning Jesus" meant that I would have to relearn how to live my life. But that's exactly what Matthew 5 does in the life of a follower of Jesus. It asks us to live life, not on a different level, but on a different plane altogether. I am faced with that challenge every time I reread his Sermon on the Mount. With his words, Jesus encourages me to look at my life in the mirror and see the way that God sees me. But not only does this passage reveal that over and over again; I also get a pretty extensive view of the kind of life he desires to see in me.

Whenever I get the picture of me in the mirror, through experiences, conversations with people, and even in my own stupidity, I get a view of what God desires. Every time I see it, it makes me wonder again how the people who actually heard Jesus utter those words reacted.

The Jewish men and women who sat there listening to Jesus on the mountain must have been overwhelmed by what Jesus showed them in the mirror. In daring them to believe in him, Jesus brought their lifestyle into question. But not only that—the words he spoke challenged more than four thousand years of their ancestral history.

I would think that Jesus' points, even those simple to comprehend, like *turn the other cheek* and *love your enemies*, would have left many in the crowd with a few follow-up questions. Matthew's depiction of the event doesn't imply that there was a Q&A session at the end of his talk. And I'm quite sure he didn't offer sermon notes or sell his talk on DVD at a merchandise table on the top of the hill.

Jesus basically looked at those people and, with a bunch of small messages rolled into one big message, said: "You're about to relearn everything you know to be true about God, because I am here to fulfill every promise that he has ever made to you."

Probably to some of them, it seemed that Jesus was asking too much of them in telling them to radically change everything they had ever learned. It's no wonder so many eventually found it hard to have faith and then ended up resisting the whole thing. If I had been there, I probably would have been one of the many who resisted him, too.

I believe I have a slight inkling of an idea what the Jewish followers must have felt when Jesus came along and challenged their ideals. When Jesus asked me to relearn him, it rubbed me the wrong way too. As pathetic as this might seem, the mere thought that I had a flawed view of Christianity would have at one time seemed like blasphemy to me.

Because I was so certain that I knew what it meant to follow Jesus, I resisted anything that looked, felt, tasted, or smelled different from what I was taught. Ultimately, Jesus wouldn't let me be. He kept pursuing me to relearn his ways, his ideals, his passions. And when I finally surrendered the first time, I was certain that Jesus would be able to make his point in one lesson. However, I *quickly* learned. Some of my friends informed me that it would take a lifetime. And after thirteen years that have included thousands of times where I have had to surrender to him again and again, I'm *still* in the process of relearning Jesus.

But, often surprising to me, I'm OK with the fact that I am still in that process. It surprised me because I like the thought of a destination. I like the idea of being able to one day arrive. But that's not the faith we live. As hard as we try to make it that way, it's not.

And even more surprising to me is the fact that I don't feel guilty about being OK with the process. In fact, I'm happy about it—not satisfied—but happy. Why? Because Jesus doesn't want me to be guilty; he wants me to keep walking with him.

When I consider the lives of Jesus' twelve disciples, I'm pretty convinced that they thought the "Christian" life was going to be much simpler than it turned out to be. By the stories they told, they obviously didn't imagine that following Jesus was going to mean that they were giving up everything that came naturally and normally to them. Even after spending a better part of three years with Jesus in the flesh, they still didn't *really* get his purpose or his teachings.

I know that feeling.

They thought they got it. Most of them seemed quite sure of their faith and reasons for following this God-man. The way they tell the story gives the impression they thought that by following Jesus for three years they had somehow *arrived* in their faith.

I know that feeling, too.

But when Jesus died, their *arrived* faith got tested. They thought it was over. They believed they were finished with their "little adventure to save the world with Jesus." What they had believed in so strongly was now gone; the place of faith they thought they had arrived at got moved, and they felt lost. And back to their fishing boats they went.

Over the years, I've heard more than a few preachers ridicule the disciples for going back to their fishing boats after Jesus died. They said something like, "Their faith was so small that they just went right back to their old way of living. How stupid can they be? Weren't they listening to Jesus when he said that he was the Messiah? I think I would have been waiting for him somewhere."

But I believe the disciples were simply being human. And I'm quite sure I would have been fishing that day too. The disciples made the same mistake I have made many times—the same mistake that this book chronicles over and over again. They assumed that the Christian faith was a destination, not a journey.

It wasn't until much later that they realized that the kind of faith Jesus desired would probably take them just a little less than a lifetime to fully understand. But they would have never realized that unless they took a chance and lived the life. Jesus wasn't looking for people who were prone to think of themselves as perfect. He didn't need people who would be quick to think they had arrived at an ideal place in their faith. He knows that if we think like this, we are putting ourselves in danger of becoming pointless, irrelevant, prideful, and legalistic. The disciples eventually learned that Jesus wanted a few humble people willing to risk their lives, dreams, and popularity on an adventure to save the world.

For years, I believed Jesus wanted me to be perfect. For years, I believed that somehow I could find a way to make myself live exactly like he describes in Matthew 5. I thought there was a destination that I was striving toward. I was looking for a place where living out the principles of Jesus would suddenly feel natural to my spirit. But slowly, I have come to know that me becoming like Jesus is indeed a journey.

And when I finally realized that this "relearning Jesus" gig was a journey, it dawned on me that when Jesus asked me to begin this gig thirteen years ago, he never said, "Oh, by the way, you have to be perfect." And he didn't look at me and promise, "If you follow me, you'll eventually know all of the answers to the questions that are running through your mind." And he didn't say, "This life is simple. You'll get it in no time."

You learn lots of these kinds of things on the journey.

The journey has taught me to have the freedom to be honest and admit imperfection; in fact, I'm free enough today to not even try to be perfect. I've learned while traveling with Jesus that I will never have all the answers to some of my big God questions. But I've learned not to let that bother me. In fact, when you can admit you don't know everything there is to know about God, humility follows. And I've learned from experience that life on the journey is hard. In fact, it feels impossible at times. But today, when I look back on the road that I have traveled on thus far, and I think about the journey that I am hoping for in the future, I think I'm OK with it being hard—although, truthfully, that sentiment comes and goes with each new encounter.

But still, I learn and relearn.

Through conversations and people, sermons and art, experiences and mistakes, tragedy and complete stupidity, I am indeed in the process of relearning Jesus. All that I experience in this life leads me to dig and pursue and wrestle, getting to know the things that Jesus loves to see come out in my life—peace, salt, light, mercy, truth, purity, humility, and love. And it's my sincere prayer that throughout my life I keep learning how to both live and experience the magic that these qualities display when they are lived out in the life of a Christian.

Why do I pursue this? Because I long for my faith experience to leave me feeling amazed by God, left in disbelief when Jesus uses me, and embarrassed every time I miss an opportunity.

The lives and stories of Brian, Lisa, Eileen, Darlene, Erin, and all the others I mentioned in this book continue to teach me what it means to relearn Jesus. They, like me, are just imperfect people struggling to stay with Jesus on the journey and surrender to the truth that our lives are not about *our* stories, but about his. Only then do we get to see some of what Jesus taught in Matthew 5 lived out in our humanity.

I continue to resist the urge to stay in one place in my faith. I'm sure that my future conversations, experiences, and stupidity will keep reminding me of that message.

I never stop looking for God to move through his people. I never get tired of seeing that. Those moments encourage me to continue on my journey. All of us need to get a taste of what Jesus meant when he said, "Blessed are …"

A follower of Jesus is simply one who refuses to stay in one place. A follower of Jesus knows that grace will catch him. A follower of Jesus is generally not interested in wealth, fame, and power. A follower of Jesus pursues making peace, showing mercy, and chasing truth. They are determined to understand what it means to be salt and what it means to be light in this world. They go after a pure heart with gusto and surrender. They know that humility is the most beautiful of traits. They try to show love at every turn in the journey, through every pothole in the road and through exhaustion from the elements that surround it.

A person who is relearning Jesus is simply one who is on a journey with him—and who, in the process of that journey, will look for an opportunity to make other people feel as if they've just experienced the love of Christ.

Also available from Matthew Paul Turner and David C. Cook:

HOKEY
Curious People Finding What Life's All About
POKEY

Introduction and chapter 1 excerpt

curious: an introduction

Not every event in our lives has profound meaning or becomes foundational for the rest of our journey. However, I believe that sometimes (at least, for me) the experiences we have and the people we encounter in this life point to a greater significance than the event itself. More than likely, all of us have had experiences that have played a role in helping us figure out a little about life. I've had several times when a book or a lecture has taught me a life lesson. But I've also learned a lot through conversations, relationships, and yes, conflict. I have come to look at certain events as road signs, leading me, or perhaps guiding me, in a good and healthy direction. All of these moments present opportunities for me to learn, grow, or experience God in my story. Sometimes it's just a small lesson that I learn—something I think about only in that moment. But once in a while an experience points to something that I am supposed to take with me for the long haul. The following conversation, though quite ordinary, has stayed with me for a long time. I'm still in the process of figuring it out.

A Curious Conversation

Despite the fact that I'd only met the man seven minutes ago, I nodded an expressive *yes* when he asked me if he could tell me a story. I didn't agree to chat because I wanted to hear his story; I agreed to it mostly because it's difficult to really say no to that kind of question. Well, I suppose it's possible, but that would require uncomfortable honesty on my part, and when you're sitting in the middle seat on a Southwest flight from BWI to LAX, any additional discomfort could be lethal.

The man I was sitting next to wore tan cargo pants and a light blue Sundance Film Festival T-shirt—something he found at a yard sale in Philly. He sported flip-flops and his hair, although mostly covered up with a baseball cap, looked greasy. Before he began to tell me his story, he shut down his laptop, told one of the flight attendants that she looked like Michelle Pfeiffer (she didn't), and as we jetted down the runway, crossed himself. I assumed that meant he was Catholic, since it seemed to be exactly what my friend Sherry did anytime she boarded a plane, drove a car, or stepped onto a bathroom scale.

Just about the time I had opened to the gossip section of *Us Weekly*—there's nothing like reading about Nicole Richie's thin addiction that makes a five-and-a-half-hour plane ride seem like the good life—the man started talking.

"I've been doing a lot of thinking lately about my life," he said, turning his head my way and looking at me with a passionate glance. "You know, man, I've been doing the kind of thinking where you can almost feel it aging you, and if you didn't know any better, you'd swear that you had become intoxicated with self-absorption. I'm probably thinking too much. Honestly, I think I was born to do that. According to Myers-Briggs, I'm an ENTP. Extrovert. Intuitive. *Thinker*. Perceiver. That's definitely me in a nutshell; I'm inclined to think God must have shot me up with an extra dose of cognitive capability. Either that or I'm just unstable. I don't know."

He laughed.

"If my father had been the kind of person to use analogies like I do, he probably would have said that I was not only intoxicated by my own thoughts, but that I was in need of therapy."

He laughed again.

"But who am I kidding?" he asked. "Dad didn't believe in therapy of any kind. Everything was black and white with him. He seemed almost incapable of seeing or believing anything that was outside the boundaries of his personal formula for life. As you can probably guess, he and I rarely understood each other, but that was mostly because all too often, I didn't support his formulas. That's always been a fault of mine. I find too much joy in being the devil's advocate, a trait that interestingly enough is quite consistent with an ENTP.

"Unfortunately, Dad died suddenly back in 1997, which is when I tried to stop caring about what he thought of me. But when I really think about it, I'm haunted by the thought that I might actually care more now about his point of view than when he was alive. Of course, that might be partly true because he's not here to argue his point. Dad was right about one thing: I do think far too much about my own existence. To be honest, I probably do it more now than I ever have. I've become consumed by the stories of my past that keep popping up in the back of my head. And you know what's really sad? Oftentimes, it's not the interesting stories that I think about. Nope. The stories that most often consume me tend to be the ones that bother me or leave me feeling empty. And isn't it awful that the stories we are obsessed with end up defining us as individuals, or worse, as sellouts? I'll never forget the time he forced me to take karate."

"Forced you to take karate?" I asked. "Why did he do that?"

"Because my father heard about one of the popular kids from my high school getting his blue belt. His *blue* belt. That was when Dad looked at me and said, 'I think you should have a blue belt too, Chas!' Of course, I was thinking, *Who frickin' cares about a blue belt?* And, naturally, the guy who ended up being Mr. Blue Belt just so happened to be the person I despised the most at my high school. The kid's name was Jeffrey Smalders. I can still hear my father's voice: 'Doesn't Jeffrey look cool all dressed up in his karate outfit, Son? Gosh, he's really built for a fifteen-year-old, huh?' He said that to me as we walked into the fire department."

"Wait. Fire department?"

"My town didn't have a YMCA or any athletic clubs. My town's fire department was the only place that had a large room that happened to also feature mirrors all along its walls. The mayor allowed karate classes to be held there on Tuesdays and Thursdays."

"Okay, I'm with you. But why were you so against taking karate? I mean, I'm not trying to be unsympathetic, but a lot of kids get forced to learn how to do a roundhouse kick."

"Yeah, that's true. But usually, kids who take karate lessons aren't athletically impaired like I was. And I was pretty much a nerd. And being good at karate wasn't going to make me cool, just like being good at karate doesn't make Steven Seagal cool, and he's lucky enough to have a story line! Besides, I was angry at my father on that first night of karate because I wanted to be home watching Ronald Reagan."

"Ronald Reagan? Why?"

"Oh, I loved everything about the Gipper—his points of view, his speaking voice, his fingernails. I've always said that Reagan should have been better known for his fingernails. They were always manicured and unbitten, a quality I think shows confidence in a person. And do you want to know what speech of his I missed? The one where he told Gorbachev to tear down the Berlin wall. It was only the most historically significant speech of his career. Gosh, that man was brave. And as far as I can tell, he didn't know one lick of karate."

"So I'm guessing you dropped out of karate pretty quickly then, eh?"

"You're getting ahead of me a bit. I'll get there."

"Sorry."

"My father went with me to that first class. You know, he seemed to think that karate was going to be the answer to all of my problems, which, for him, included my joy of reading and my ineptness with all things athletic. 'This night might very well change your life, Chas.' That's what he told me as I stood in my underwear in the fire department's locker room and changed into my uniform. The first hour was pretty boring; I learned some stretching and exercise techniques. I said to Dad, 'Isn't this pretty much yoga?' But then came hour two when I had the pleasure of sitting on the sideline of a blue mat and watching Jeffrey Smalders kick everyone's butt. 'Look at how high Jeffrey can kick, Chas!' my dad said to me while he sat there beside me, gawking at Jeffrey's skill as I imagined the spectators in ancient Rome had as they watched lions pounce on and eat small children. 'Go, Jeff! Kick him, man! Don't let him score another point! Look out! Jeff, get him! Yes! Good job!' That moment was humiliating for me; it was like I was watching what a father-son relationship was supposed to be."

"Wow," I said. "That's hard, man. Did you ever say anything to your father? Did you tell him how that situation made you feel?"

"No! I didn't say anything. Instead of talking, I decided that the best possible retaliation against preppy boy and his little cheerleader friend—*my father*—would be to try and deny my thoughts, deny being uncoordinated, deny my love for reading, and for once in my life take on my father's need for me to be talented at something physical."

"You felt like you needed to prove something, huh?"

"Yes."

"Oh, I think I know what you were feeling, bro. It was like in *that* moment you knew what you had to do—who you had to be to earn his approval."

"That's right."

"And since you were only fifteen, it probably felt pretty big to you."

"Like a boulder in my gut."

"And as a way of pursuing your father's respect, I'm sure that somewhere in the back of your mind you were constructing a plot to kick Jeffrey Smalders' butt in karate."

"That was God's plan, bro. As I sat on that hard cold floor and watched Jeffrey spar and my father cheer, whistle, and make verbal love to my archrival, I wanted Jeffrey to feel a little humiliation for once. I would defeat him for every young man in the class of 1989 who had ever felt the sting of being put in their athletic place by Smalders. I would defeat him for every young woman who had ever been lured into lust-filled thoughts by his bulky biceps and his chiseled chest. It was like something had begun to roar inside me. But that was only happening in my imagination; in real life, I was no Captain America. Heck, I wasn't even Ralph Macchio. I was more like Linus."

"Dang, man. So did you go back to karate class the following week?"

"I did."

"To make your statement."

"I guess."

"Did you ever end up getting your blue belt?"

"Nope."

"Green belt?"

"Nope. I got my brown."

"Wow, man. You went one level further than blue. That's awesome. I mean, that's what you wanted to do; so that's cool that you actually accomplished what you set out to do. Most people only dream of getting to that place."

"Yep, I invested every part of my being into karate. I was

fueled by the weight inside of me to prove myself to the people of my town—to set myself apart from the ordinary small-town kid. Well, that, and the desire to hear my father cheer for me the way he cheered for Jeffrey. I cared about that, too."

"So, he must have been pleased when you finally got your blue belt and then went on to get your brown, huh?"

"He was happy."

"And did you ever get the chance to spar with Jeffrey?"

"Five times."

"And did you win?"

"I beat him once. The last time we sparred. It was the last match before the two of us graduated, and on that evening I came at him with a vengeance. By that time, Jeffrey was already on his second-level black belt. He was quicker, stronger, and more athletic than me. Still, that night I made everyone at the fire department forget about all of that. It was my night. And believe me, the adrenaline was pumping, man. Coach told me that Jeffrey and I were essentially tied going into the third match. He said I needed to block more and remain balanced. I became extremely focused, and Jeffrey never scored a point during that last match. He was so humiliated by losing that he walked off the mat holding back tears and went right to the locker room. I didn't even get a chance to say anything to him. People were screaming. My father was jumping up and down. He ran onto the mat and hugged me. He told me he was proud of me. It was an interesting night, for sure."

"So you proved yourself!" I said, drinking the last sip of my watered-down cranberry-flavored Sprite. "That must have made you feel amazing. Finally, the good guy beat the crap out of the preppy kid who thought he was better than everyone else."

"Actually, I felt horrible. Sure, I'd won, but when I thought about all that I had given up to get to that spot, I wasn't sure it was worth it."

"You weren't the least bit excited about winning? How is that possible? I mean, you were only a brown belt—the underdog—and you beat Jeffrey, the pompous guy who humiliated everyone? Dude, do you know how many guys would kill for that kind of movie ending? It had to feel a little rewarding. And not to mention, you proved to your father that you had what it takes. Isn't that what life's all about, proving you can do the seemingly impossible? Making everyone you know stop in their tracks and for once notice you? To some extent, that had to feel good!"

"Sure, there was a small part of me that was cheering on the inside," he said, looking at me, and giving me a halfhearted grin. "But it would have been much more impressive for me to have just been myself and not become something I wasn't made to be."

He stopped talking for a moment, and then added, "You know, man, the problem is, most of the time embracing who you were made to be doesn't usually make you popular, and it rarely makes you cool. But you learn that. At least, I did. Even today, I think most of the time I feel just curious enough to be dangerous."

Curious People

Chas is perhaps the most interesting stranger I've ever met on a plane. Vulnerable. Cocky. Obsessive. Emotional. A pilgrim. The thirtysomething had rather insightful observations about his life, from his relationship with his father to his pseudo-knowledge about Myers-Briggs. Sadly, the story he shared was about a man who was still struggling with the fact that he had to become something he wasn't meant to be in order to earn the approval of his father. But that's not what I remember most about Chas. As I walked off the plane, I could not seem to forget his use of the word *curious*. It stuck out for some reason. I kept replaying its meaning and implications over and over again in my head. I thought about how often it gets used in a negative connotation and how ridiculous that is. Think about it: Being curious—to be eager or filled with wonder about something—is a beautiful concept. That's especially true in relationship to our calling.

That's why I think we should be curious. I think it should be something we're always pursuing. I think those who experience life are almost always curious people. They're filled with an odd desire to figure out the *why* and *when* and *how* of their story. I'm not only talking about people who are famous, popular, rich, intelligent, or successful. A curious person could be anybody—anybody who's willing to put a little effort into finding out what life is about. I hope this book will share some stories and provide some insights on what it means to pursue the curious path.

My Questions for You

1. Do you ever contemplate how everyday events like meeting strangers on planes or having random conversations at coffeehouses affect you?

2. How have your relationships with your family members empowered or weakened your pursuit of your true passions?

3. Have you ever felt like you have become "unlike yourself" in order to please somebody else?

4. What are you truly curious about?

a curious path

No story is the same to us after a lapse of time; or rather we who read it are no longer the same interpreters.

—GEORGE ELIOT

We Need True Stories

I learned at a very young age the importance of listening to people's stories. My father is a fantastic storyteller. Most of his stories are from his youthful past, growing up on a dairy farm in the 1940s. When I was a child, right before bedtime, Dad would come into my room, sit on my bed, and tell me one of his curious tales as a youngster. His stories had plot. They had mischief. And they always had a moral—one that he wanted me to learn. Now that I am older, I value all of his stories, even the silly ones. I believe they are a part of me in some way. They are my history, my roots, and I hold on to them as I navigate my way through this curious life I've been given. But perhaps the most valuable part of Dad telling me his stories is that he gave me permission to fall asleep imagining and dreaming about my own story. In other words, his stories helped me find my path.

Hearing people's stories encourages us to contemplate our own stories, which often have something to tell us about what our calling is about. And so our stories point to our calling, while our calling sheds some light on the *how* and *what* of our stories. But how do we even begin to find our calling or, if you will, the meaning of our stories? I think one of the ways is by paying attention to our lives and the stories around us, letting them sink in, and hopefully, allowing them to direct us onto a good path.

Believe me, I realize that discovering your calling isn't a simple task. However, it's something that each of us desires to figure out. One of the ways that I personally have connected to my own calling is by carrying with me (figuratively, not literally) a collection of true stories—not just of my own personal experiences, but stories from my family's past, stories that I've read or heard, and stories that have moved me out of my comfort zone. A lot of these stories come from people who have lived a lot longer than I have and who are much wiser.

Life Is Sometimes Unfair

In 1986, when I was only thirteen, my sister Kelley got a job at the local nursing home as an activities coordinator. Though Magnolia Hall was an above-average elder-care facility, Kelley's job consisted of distracting the residents with crafts so they wouldn't realize where they were. Believe it or not, she was successful sometimes. Although the craft projects she organized often did the trick, residents most often forgot their whereabouts when the task at hand involved gambling.

Every Tuesday and Thursday at 2:00 p.m., if a resident wasn't blind, dead, or Baptist, they gathered in the nursing home's cafeteria for an hour's worth of unadulterated, cutthroat bingo. And believe me, those nursing-home folk took their bingo playing very seriously. I was always excited when my sister let me volunteer during bingo hour. Probably more than most adolescents my age, I really enjoyed helping old people do things. For me, helping the elderly was much more fulfilling than helping people who could help themselves. Perhaps I live in some sick kind of reality, but it was always easier for me to understand a Christian's calling to be the hands and feet of God in the world when Kelley assigned my hands to assist Mr. Calkins, the old man who had no arms. I'd often heard my pastor preach against the woes of bingo, but I couldn't understand why when I considered Magnolia Hall's bingo hour. Each week, I saw a glimpse of God in the face of limbless Mr. Calkins. God seemed to show up every time Mr. Calkins borrowed my appendages to place a bingo chip, clap between games, or wipe the snot from his nose.

One afternoon, after bingo was finished, I wheeled Mr. Calkins back to his room. As I pushed him up hallway after hallway, he talked constantly. "Young man, I haven't had my arms for almost five years," he said, his voice chronically raspy. "I lost them because of poor circulation. And do you know that even though it has been that long, I have never gotten used to not having arms. At least four or five times a day, I reach for something. Or at least I try to reach for something. I can't seem to remember that I ain't got no hands. It's frustrating."

Mr. Calkins' story moved me. In some ways, it still moves me. I felt sorry for him. I didn't understand why life was so unfair. I hated it. I guess at the time, I thought that if you lost something important like your arms, the part of your brain that maneuvers the lost members should go too. But often the opposite is true. Instead of forgetting about what you no longer have, you're usually tempted to think about it more. That's why Mr. Calkins' story, though rather simple, became one I carry around with me. Watching him interact with the other residents despite what he didn't have was inspiring. "You have to look past what you lost or never had to begin with and grab on to the things that you *do* have," he told me. "You can't live in the past, Son."

I don't know about you, but I need to be reminded of what's true sometimes. And sometimes that truth comes from these kinds of ordinary moments—conversations and experiences that remind me of what's important. I learned from Mr. Calkins that I didn't want to focus on what I didn't have or the stuff that I had lost along the way, but instead, on what God had given to me in the here and now.

HOKEY MOMENT

Spend a minute or two thinking of one story that you've heard or experienced that has continued to impact your life.

Does it seem to you that true stories are becoming less and less important to people today? And when I say "true," I don't simply mean something that happened, but rather, stories that lead us to discover truth—perhaps truth about ourselves or about our futures or about our careers. I happen to think that as time goes on, we're hearing fewer and fewer true stories.

I think one of the reasons this has happened is because a lot of us have grown accustomed to most of the stories we hear being doctored up or exaggerated to some degree. In other words, we've let the media and other cultural elements tell us who we should be and how we should live for so long that we often end up feeling like our own stories aren't exciting enough or dramatic enough or sexy enough. So we resist sharing them.

It's quite sad that we as a culture have somewhere along the line become accustomed to hearing and experiencing untrue stories. More than likely, most of us have heard more than a few muted stories on Sunday mornings. We've watched sensationalized ones at the movie theater on Friday nights. And consequently, some of us have exaggerated our own. I will admit that things like special effects, punch lines, and clever storytelling have made some stories exciting and entertaining, but I also think these storytelling techniques have caused a lot of people to stop pursuing their own true stories, often deeming them not important or attractive enough.

I think a lot of us have an addiction to the exaggerated, the processed, the untrue. I believe we're addicted to these kinds of stories the same way we're addicted to caffeine, prescription drugs, and cigarettes. And here's the sad part: I think sometimes those kinds of stories are just as harmful to our health. Our dependence on sensationalism and/or blandness has made the true stories about people—you know, the ones that sometimes have the ability to beckon us out of life's holes with a little hope, seem boring or unmoving to us. Again, I think that's sad, because humans learn by way of narrative. Stories teach us how to live. And if all the stories we hear have been processed to some degree, how are we supposed to truly connect with what our calling might be? How can we find the path toward figuring out life if all we're living in is an unreal world?

The stories of people—realistic ones about regular people living true lives—help us discover our own stories. But what so many of us do not realize is this: The stories we pay attention to end up shaping us. In most instances we become what we believe to be true. Think I'm exaggerating? Look at how many young women are obsessed with their weight and are dieting because they believe "true beauty" is a size two. (It's not, by the way.) And, likewise, consider how many men give their lives over to their jobs because they've grown up in a culture that tells them true success requires them to make $150,000 or more a year. See the danger in untrue stories? They can affect our futures far more than most of us realize.

Calling Is a Path

Hokey Pokey is about getting on a path toward discovering what life is about. Notice that the subtitle to this book does not say "people who have found what life is about." That's because it's not about people who think they've arrived! It's about people who are in the process of discovery. This curious path toward figuring out life is not one that ends. Oh, it's possible to stray off the right path from time to time. And you can get lost. And it's even possible to think you're on the right road when you're not. But don't think of calling as something that you arrive at—because it's not. It's a journey that takes a lifetime. It's a process. And it's important to remember that, no matter who we are or where we are on the path, we are always in process.

I tend to think that most people desire to know what life is about, or at least, have some kind of curiosity about it. For most of us, it's an inner craving, like the need for a good friend or a good conversation or a good foreign beer. I tend to think we want to be in the know about life because we humans are nosy creatures; some of us are hopelessly in love with that feeling of exclusivity that comes when we are in the know about all kinds of stuff, but especially life.

Isn't that why we put so much effort into figuring life out? Those who do, I believe, are brave. I think it takes a healthy dose of curiosity and wonder to lead us onto a journey toward discovering a little meaning in this life. And unfortunately, the path toward doing so isn't easy. Like I said in the introduction, I'm not just talking about the path toward the bigger meaning—everything big and small is somehow sacred—I'm also talking about the kind of meaning that is found in the most ordinary and human parts of life: like in relationships, serving, the jobs we have, and other things that make us smile.

In a nutshell, we crave to know our calling. I think it's a desire that God has given us. Not everyone believes that to be true, but I do. When I read Scripture, I am moved by the stories of men and women who passionately believed they were on earth for a greater purpose. They believed in things that were bigger than themselves. They believed they were called by God to live and do his work. Those of us who follow Jesus carry on that tradition. We believe we are God's children and that we, too, are called to something bigger than what we can see. We are God's hands. We are his feet. And while he is constantly redeeming the story of this world through his Son, Jesus, we are called to join him in that narrative, to look for our places in the story and participate in the work he is doing.

But our beliefs can often make the journey toward knowing the *how* and *why* of this life very complicated. But for some reason, God has given each of us a desire to know something about our meaning, a curiosity that keeps us moving toward figuring life out. And though the road is rocky, the truth is that sometimes the path toward learning the big and small of life's meaning makes us into who we are. In other words, the "process" can teach us something if we allow it to. People who pursue life with an inquisitive spirit sometimes find answers to all or some of those questions: *Why am I here? What am I supposed to do with my life? How can I know if I'm on the right path? Is God involved in my story? Does God even care about me?*

We live in a culture where an awful lot of people want life's answers to come easy and processed so that they're quick to understand. A friend of mine (I'll call him Jason) really enjoys answering people's big questions. No matter what the question—real or rhetorical—he will offer his two cents to anyone about almost any topic. People call him Kramer behind his back because they're convinced that he thinks of himself as the "expert" in almost any situation. And he does always have an easy answer.

"I'm just confused," said the girl, who was a friend of a friend who had joined Jason and me for drinks after work one Tuesday night. I forget exactly what her comment was in reference to, but I think it had to do with her not being married. Or maybe it was about sex. All I remember is that she was confused about something.

"Sometimes I just don't get how I am supposed to *hear* God," she said. "People tell me all the time that I'm supposed to, and I don't believe I've ever heard him."

Most of us around the table just nodded our heads. One person offered, "I think a lot of us are with you there. That's a hard topic for sure."

"Well, have you heard about the four Ps of interacting with God?" asked Jason.

"I don't think so," she said, giving him her complete attention.

"It's easy!" said Jason. "Prepare. Pray. Persist. Promise. I learned this from a pastor back in Jersey. It's just an easy way for me to remember that, when I need answers, I need to get quiet, talk to God, be consistent about talking to God, and then lean on the promises found in his Word. Never fails!"

"And you hear God answer you using this method?"

"Most of the time, and when I don't hear him, I just assume he's telling me no."

Don't you just love when people try to simplify God this way? These kinds of people take something that could potentially be *p*recious, *p*ersonal, *p*assionate, and maybe a little *p*erplexing and make it seem about as deep as *Sesame Street*. The truth is, the answers to the grandiose questions that we have about life aren't easy to find, and I think this is okay. We shouldn't want the answers to be easy. Easy means we're not willing to get dirty. Easy means we're not embracing life's mysteries. And often, easy means we're living somebody else's story rather than seeking what God would have for us as individuals.

No wonder there are a wealth of people giving easy answers to life's most difficult questions. When I hear some of the perfect four-point solutions that professionals write about in books and project on

PowerPoint displays at seminars, it makes me kind of nauseous. Why am I so distraught by the easy answers? For starters, they are too simple, too processed, too one-size-fits-all. And just as I don't believe we are meant to digest "food" made by Kraft or Campbell's, I don't think we are meant to live within the confines of somebody else's processed path. That's not how we were created, and yet, we still continue to seek the next easy solution because we don't want to do the hard work it takes to lose weight, heal a relationship, or find our dream job. We would rather get what we want in four easy steps. For only $13.99. But we suffer consequences when we embrace such easy *microwavable* answers.

C. S. Lewis said that we are all souls who live and breathe and feel and respond to story. The easy answers may have been sufficient for us at one time in our lives, but they aren't good enough for us right now. Life's big questions do not have easy answers. And that's okay. The easy answers don't consider our passions and desires—the very core of our beings. And we have to consider who we are as individuals when we are talking about something as important as what we were made to do in this world.

My Questions for You

1. Think of someone you have a great deal of respect for in your life. What do you admire about his or her journey that you would like to apply to your own?

2. Have you ever been offered an easy answer to a complicated question? How did this make you feel?

No doubt, calling is a strange topic. When you think about it, there are an awful lot of inconsistencies and uncertainties when it comes to understanding what calling even means. For instance, if I were to ask a hundred people to define their idea of "calling," there's a better-than-average chance that I could get a hundred different answers. Whether our comprehension about calling is limited or flawed or incorrect or perhaps just misconstrued and in process, the topic seems to leave a large portion of the population befuddled.

If that's you, it might help you to know that you're not alone. I think our misunderstandings with calling are kind of normal and maybe even warranted to some degree. Without great amounts of research and experiential study, a person trying to grasp the idea of calling might feel similar to those who started tuning into *Lost* at any point after the second episode. (I don't know about you, but I think the appropriateness of that show's title is astounding.) But I guess that's what makes calling such an interesting topic—one that has throughout time caused people to form a multitude of different opinions about what it entails and how it's discovered. The range of ideas surrounding calling often leaves me perplexed (which quite honestly, isn't some great feat), but that happens mainly because one individual's calling might be another person's way of making ends meet. And, while some people believe they exist *within* their calling, that their entire reason for living is mandated by an invisible and universal force they may call God, others think their calling is something they work toward, that it's something they arrive at or pursue. And, I'm quite sure that some people come up with their own rather imaginative combo of those explanations.

There is a good amount of confusion and fear and uncertainty around calling. It's nobody's fault; I think perplexity is a part of the very nature of the concept. After all, calling is a mystery. For some, the definition of *calling* has to include the question of why we exist, and as you might expect, the answer to that question isn't simple. Quite frankly, even when put in the simplest of terms, each of our answers depends largely on our personal experience and how we interpret that experience.

Some of us like to paint this great mystic picture of personal calling, one that is spiritual and supernatural; others believe the concept of calling is something that we can easily understand—to the point where formulas and surveys can answer any questions we have about the subject. One of the more popular ways of thinking about our calling helms on the idea that calling is about *doing* as opposed to *being*. Made up of an individual's core values, responsibilities, and passions, the more logical thinkers among us suggest that our callings play out in various forms such as employment, family, social standard, and religion. And that's not exactly incorrect thinking.

My personal experience with trying to figure out my calling is that it's sometimes a rather dysfunctional journey, one that ebbs and flows and malfunctions at inappropriate times. And quite honestly, I learned to think of that as a good thing. At least, that's true today. Because that's how we learn, that's how our stories get written—by way of the process or the path. It kind of reminds me of the Chevy Celebrity I owned in college. It was white with blue interior and had a torn off Bush/Quayle '92 sticker on its bumper. Granted, the car almost always *eventually* got me to where I wanted to go, but upon arriving at my destination, those who rode with me promptly exited the car and kissed the ground. Still, I often felt a sense of accomplishment—like I had earned that trip. Sure, some of my friends had arrived twenty or thirty minutes earlier in their BMWs or Geo Trackers, but they arrived without a story to tell. Even though that old car of mine left me feeling frustrated on many occasions, I felt a bit of thrill in never knowing what would take place between where I was and where I was going to end up.

Here's what I've learned: The journey toward figuring out our calling is a little bumpy. But I've also learned that more often than not there's something true to hold on to in just embracing the adventure of the search, in engaging the story of what God is doing or desires to be doing in our lives. No, the story I encounter might not be an epic—but honestly, no matter what John Eldredge might suggest, sometimes epics are overrated (did you see *Alexander*?). But you know, while I may get to experience an epic from time to time, sometimes I just want my life to resemble a limerick, something short but true that makes only a little sense but gives me something to talk and laugh about with friends and strangers. And of course, it should rhyme! The curious path begins with you being willing to focus a little attention on your own story—not in an egocentric manner, but in a way that makes you get honest with yourself so that you will begin to know who you are, what you're good at, and how God fits into your narrative.

I think a lot of times, many of us are too frightened by the adventure that comes with searching, mostly because we're afraid of where it might lead or, scarier still, where it won't. I've certainly had moments in my life when I've resisted the search, choosing rather to sit on my backside in front of the TV and watch somebody else's "adventure," or at least ABC or NBC's overproduced version of somebody's adventure. Many people know what I'm talking about too. Sadly, sometimes watching thirty minutes of somebody else's woes is a lot easier (and much more entertaining, frankly) than jetting out and experiencing my own.

But people who sit on couches and watch exaggerated versions of other people's stories miss out on hearing, learning, seeing, or experiencing something true for their own story. Not every true experience is good or valid to what's happening in our lives, yet once in a while, we encounter something true that changes our lives or maybe simply changes our day. It's just another mile on the path toward becoming who we're meant to be. Again, it's a process, and finding what life is really all about begins with being brave enough to become curious.

My Questions for You

1. How do you define calling?
2. Is the topic of calling confusing for you? If your answer is yes, why? If your answer is no, how do you see your personal calling?